SAVING BLOOD

How you can have the power of God's grace in your life

KEAVIN HAYDEN
with
DAVID MERRILL

Pacific Press® Publishing Association
Nampa, Idaho
Oshawa, Ontario, Canada

**A Note About the Use in this Book of the Spirit of Prophecy
as Manifested in the Writings of Ellen G. White**

All doctrine clearly should be established and delineated from the Word of God. The use of Ellen White's writings in this book is intended to affirm and play a supporting role to what is already established throughout the pages of Holy Writ. As the lesser light, it is intended to stimulate our appetite for the nuggets of divine truth that lie buried in the pages of the Bible. This is the functional purpose of Mrs. White's writings as they relate to the Bible. Their place is to jumpstart our neglect and indifference toward the Bible that often is the result of simply not knowing how to begin investigating biblical truth. Just as a master craftsman inspires an apprentice by familiarizing him with the tools and tricks of the trade, so the lifework of Ellen White is intended to better familiarize us with authentic biblical principles and teachings. Her writings are not designed to do our thinking for us but to help teach us how to think for ourselves in the biblical context.

Edited by B. Russell Holt
Designed by Dennis Ferree
Cover photo by Sinclair Studio

ISBN 0-8163-1767-4

00 01 02 03 04 • 5 4 3 2 1

ARE YOU WASHED IN THE BLOOD?

Have you been to Jesus for the cleansing pow'r?
Are you washed in the blood of the Lamb?
Are you fully trusting in His grace this hour?
Are you washed in the blood of the Lamb?

Are you walking daily by the Saviour's side?
Are you washed in the blood of the Lamb?
Do you rest each moment in the Crucified?
Are you washed in the blood of the Lamb?

When the Bridegroom cometh will your robes be white?
Are you washed in the blood of the Lamb?
Will your soul be ready for the mansions bright?
And be washed in the blood of the Lamb?

Lay aside the garments that are stained with sin.
Are you washed in the blood of the Lamb?
There's a fountain flowing for the soul unclean,
Oh, be washed in the blood of the Lamb!

Are you washed
in the blood,
In the soul-cleansing blood of the Lamb?
Are your garments spotless?
Are they white as snow?
Are you washed in the blood of the Lamb?
—Elisha A. Hoffman

"It is the darkness of misapprehension of God that is enshrouding the world. Men are losing their knowledge of His character. It has been misunderstood and misinterpreted. At this time a message from God is to be proclaimed, a message illuminating in its influence and saving in its power. His character is to be made known. . . the last message of mercy to be given to the world is a revelation of His character of love" (*Christ's Object Lessons*, 415).

" 'And this is life eternal, that they might know thee the only true God, and Jesus Christ, whom thou hast sent' " (John 17:3).

CONTENTS

INTRODUCTION

I awoke startled. Knowing I had an early morning flight, I quickly rolled over and looked at the alarm clock to see if I had overslept. Realizing I had plenty of time, I lay back on the pillow to contemplate my day.

Outside my bedroom window, almost three feet of snow lay on the Michigan landscape. I lay in my warm bed dreaming of a tropical adventure. But today it was no dream! In just a few hours I would be boarding a plane in Grand Rapids bound for the Pacific island of Guam, where I had been invited to be the speaker for a week of spiritual emphasis.

I paused in the kitchen for a quick bite of breakfast.

"Keavin, its time to go," called my wife. "Do you have everything?"

"Of course I have everything," I replied.

"Well, it doesn't hurt to double check," she insisted.

"OK. Let me see . . . Bible, notes, suitcase, plane tickets, sunglasses. Yep, everything I need!"

"Are you sure you have everything?" my wife asked again.

"Yes, Lisa. I have everything. Now let's go."

Pulling up to the terminal an hour later, I turned to kiss my children Goodbye. This is always the hardest part of traveling.

Stepping out of the truck, my trusty wife handed me my briefcase and said, "Now, are you sure . . . ?"

"Yes, Lisa," I cut her off. "I have everything. I'll call you when I get there. I love you. Bye!"

I waved as I watched my personal treasures pull away. Then I turned to enter the airport and my long-awaited excursion.

"Next!" called the ticket agent. I stepped up to the counter. "Checking two bags all the way to Guam?"

"That's right," I replied.

"May I see your passport, please?"

"Sure . . . Wait a minute! Passport? I don't need a passport, do I? I mean, isn't Guam a U.S. territory? I don't need a passport to go to Guam!"

"You are traveling through Tokyo, Mr. Hayden. You'll need your passport to get through the terminal there."

"Oh no!" I wailed. "I can't believe it! I forgot my passport! Please, isn't there something we can do? My wife just dropped me off and left. I live over an hour away, and the plane leaves in thirty minutes. Please! Please! I *have* to be in Guam!"

"I'm sorry," came the dreaded reply, "I can't even check you in without a passport."

Thanks to a friend who was willing to break into my office and drive to the airport with my passport, I was finally able to catch a later flight. But now, my original plans were all scrambled. Now I had to stay overnight in both Chicago and Tokyo, delaying my arrival in Guam by nearly two days.

A passport. Such a small, simple, inexpensive, *important* thing!

It's amazing how God has a lesson for us in every experience of life. All the way to Guam I kept thinking about how important that passport was. Then I thought how we are also going to need a passport in order to take that future flight to the Paradise of heaven. We can have our suitcases packed with all kinds of good works, yet if we forget the passport, the angelic ticket agents won't even be able to check us in for the flight.

But what is this passport? And how do we get it?

Our passport to that eternal world is none other than Jesus Christ. "He that hath the Son hath life; and he that hath not the Son of God hath not life" (1 John 5:12).

Christ's credentials by which He can issue us this escape to Paradise is the obedient life He wrought out in human flesh. The ink used to print our eternal passports is His very own saving blood. And just as my wife was concerned that I have a checklist in preparation for my trip, so God challenges us to "examine" our lives continually to see "whether . . . [we] be in the faith" (2 Corinthians 13:5).

Of course, the devil wants to ruin our eternal vacation. He is determined that none of us make that heavenly flight. He seeks to do this either by perverting our understanding of God's character, so that we have no desire to go home with Him, or he cleverly deceives us through vain philosophy and leads us to neglect securing our passport—the righteousness of Jesus.

As I combine my literary efforts with those of my good friend David Merrill, our purpose is to make Jesus Christ the central hope of all who read this book. In these pages we will try to view the issues of the great controversy from a heavenly perspective, thus revealing God's "character, government, and purposes" (*The Great Controversy*, 593). Such understanding will enable us to more intelligently fight the "good fight" of faith (2 Timothy 4:7) in the power of Christ's redeeming merits. Through these pages we will get a better glimpse of God's design to save the human race as seen "in the face of Jesus Christ" (2 Corinthians 4:6).

It is the prayer of its authors that *Saving Blood* will accomplish the purposes for which it is sent.

Keavin Hayden
January 31, 2000

CHAPTER

1

The God of the Golden Rule

From the beginning, God's means of governing has been the influence of His own righteous character. In other words, He governs His subjects without coercion or manipulation, solely by leading them with His own gracious example of right doing.

That's the way it was in heaven prior to Lucifer's rebellion. God's government rested upon His divine law, the basis of which was the principle of the golden rule. An individual angel did not have to be continually absorbed in taking care of his own needs, because his own personal well-being was the priority of all the angels around him. This law freed each angel to look not upon his own things but rather upon the things of others (see Philippians 2:4). Such a harmonious arrangement was preserved and made possible only by the unselfish example of God, who was the supreme servant of all. All was harmonious and peaceful as long as every angel focused on God's marvelous golden-rule example of making the well-being of others a top priority.

But "there was war in heaven" (Revelation 12:7). The peace of Paradise was interrupted as Lucifer pursued self-exaltation by seeking to make himself the "center of influence" in the government of God (*Testimonies for the Church*, 6:236). Satan's self-seeking led him to reject the golden rule. He repudiated the great law that "none of us liveth to himself" (Romans 14:7). He said in his heart, "I will be like the most High" (Isaiah 14:14).

This cherished desire of the creature to equal his Creator was the original sin. It naturally led Satan to imagine he could achieve a state of holiness within himself apart from Christ. It was by arousing this same desire in our first parents that he led them to sever their relationship from God in Eden. He promised them, "ye shall be as gods" (Genesis 3:5). But eating from the forbidden tree was only the *fruit* of sin. The real root was once again found in the creature choosing apostasy. Apostasy always results as the creature aspires to equal the state of the Creator's holiness or to obtain righteousness apart from Him. It naturally leads to a "falling away" from total dependence upon God (see 2 Thessalonians 2:1-12).

In conceiving that he could "be like the most High" (Isaiah 14:14), Lucifer was actually deceiving himself. He didn't really want to be "like" God in character. Instead, he coveted only the power of God's personal influence, the Lord's key to exercising divine authority within the established government. So in an attempt to destroy God's influence, the rebel angel projected upon Christ characeristics that, in reality, were the characteristics of his own state of being. Satan maintained "that God was not just in laying laws and rules upon the inhabitants of heaven; that in requiring submission and obedience from His creatures, He was seeking merely the exaltation of Himself" (*The Great Controversy*, 498). He "accused God of requiring self-denial of the angels, when He knew nothing of what it meant Himself, and when *He would not Himself make any self-sacrifice for others*. This was the accusation that Satan made against God in heaven; and after the evil one was expelled from heaven, he continually charged the Lord *with exacting service which He would not render Himself*" (*Selected Messages*, 1:406, 407).

In short, Satan claimed that God was a fraud, that He didn't live up to His own golden-rule law. He complained that the Lord was using the services of everyone else only for His own selfish purposes. He suggested that as the Infinite One, God was out of touch and couldn't fully identify with His created beings or truly know what it was like to be in their place. Posing as an insider who was privy to the internal workings of the divine government, Lucifer feigned to leak a scandal of corruption in heaven's capitol. Thus angels were deceived by his propaganda tactics.

The earth was dark

As this great controversy spread to our world, the human race also became infected by such perverted views about God. Herein lies the root of all this world's chaotic problems. It has no correct conception of God's character nor His means of governing. "And the world knew him not" (John 1:10).

> The earth was dark through misapprehension of God. That the gloomy shadows might be lightened, that the world might be brought back to God, Satan's deceptive power was to be broken. This could not be done by force. *The exercise of force is contrary to the principles of God's government*; He desires only the service of love; and love cannot be commanded; it cannot be won by force or authority. *Only by love is love awakened.* To know God is to love Him; His character must be manifested in contrast to the character of Satan. This work only one Being in all the universe could do. Only He who knew the height and depth of the love of God could make it known. Upon the world's dark night the Sun of Righteousness must rise, "with healing in His wings." Mal. 4:2 (*The Desire of Ages*, 22, italics supplied).

"Christ came to the world to meet these [Satan's] false accusations, and to reveal the Father" (*Selected Messages*, 1:407).

Yes, the revelation of Himself, as seen in the life and death of Christ, is the means by which God intends to correct the sins that are becoming increasingly displayed in the realms of this fallen world. This revelation of God's character is to be our mightiest weapon in the warfare against sin and corruption, because it is in harmony with the principles of His governing influence. The Savior said "And I, if I be lifted up from the earth, will *draw* [through His righteous influence] all men unto me" (John 12:32).

Just as the Father exalted the Son before the angelic hosts at the beginning of the great controversy as He attempted to secure their allegiance, so now He seeks to win our loyalty by uplifting Christ on the cross for our contemplation. (See *The Story of Redemption,* 13-15). This is the only hope of reformation here at the end of time—not only for the world but for the church as well.

> The purity, the holiness of the life of Jesus as presented from the Word of God, possesses more power to reform and transform the character than do all the efforts put forth in picturing the sins and crimes of men and the sure results. One steadfast look to the Saviour uplifted upon the cross will do more to purify the mind and heart from every defilement than will all the scientific explanations by the ablest tongues (*The Paulson Collection of Ellen G. White Letters, 1985*).

As a result of His genuine love, God has allowed us freedom of choice to serve Him or not to serve Him. It has always been through an appreciation of His goodness that God's faithful subjects have rendered obedience to His will, as is revealed in His law. Attempting to use fear, manipulation, or any other form of coercion to bring conviction upon the sinner's heart will never completely seal a decision for Christ. As the saying goes, "A man convinced against his will is of the same opinion still." Only by seeing God's goodness will a soul be led to genuine repentance and choose freely to serve Him.

Satan, on the other hand, must rely upon coercion and deceitful methods of manipulating the will in order to gain homage to himself. This is because he has no inherent righteous qualities by which to draw others to himself.

Satan employs two primary strategies in seeking to accomplish his purposes. He uses fear tactics, portraying God as a harsh, arbitrary taskmaster who demands our obedience, or he tries to convince us that God's kingdom of love is so jellylike in nature that we may do as we please and still be a part of it. In other words, Satan uses both fear and a false freedom as motivations to worship God. Such are the baseline principles of creature worship, which nearly the entire Christian world is now standing ready to acknowledge as the authentic religion of God. And what will happen to those who refuse to bow down to this concept of religion? That's right, Satan will then attempt to force them to submit through persecution.

God's strategy

Many haved wondered why God did not immediately put an end to Lucifer and his rebellion as soon as it began. But had He done this, Lucifer's charge that God was self-serving and arbitrary would have been plausible. God Himself would have stepped outside the boundaries of His own golden rule. Such action would not have put down the insurrection, but, rather, it would have established it in the hearts of many who witnessed marshall law being enforced. The use of force would have transformed God into the same mold as those "beast" powers described in the Bible as demanding allegiance on pain of death. Mutinous attitudes would have gone underground and would never have felt free to express their real sentiments openly concerning God and His universal government. "If God had exercised His power to punish this chief rebel, *disaffected angels would not have been manifested*; hence, God took another course, for He would manifest distinctly to all the heavenly host His justice and His judgment" (*The Story of Redemption*, 17).

As a result, God would have had to rule by police action, and His kingdom would be eternally subjected to revolt. Divine wisdom had no such purpose. So God has simply allowed the rebellion to develop fully in the eyes of every citizen of the universe so that all might see its nature. This has been necessary in order that "the thoughts of many hearts may be revealed" (Luke 2:35).

In playing out the great controversy, an eternal distinction is being made between God's governing principles as opposed to Satan's methods. Notice the following statement:

> God could have destroyed Satan and his sympathizers as easily as one can cast a pebble to the earth; but He did not do this. Rebellion was not to be overcome by force. Compelling power is found only under Satan's government. The Lord's principles are not of this order. His authority rests upon goodness, mercy, and love; and *the presentation of these principles is the means to be used.* God's government is moral, and truth and love are to be the prevailing power. It was God's purpose to place things on an eternal basis of security, and in the councils of heaven it was decided that time must be given for Satan to develop the principles which were the foundation of his system of government. He had claimed that these were superior to God's principles. Time was given for the working of Satan's principles, that they might be seen by the heavenly universe (*The Desire of Ages*, 759, italics supplied).

This is the strategy God has chosen to prove that Satan's charges are false and that His divine plan of governing is best. He maintains the moral free will of His creatures. He will not force them to choose Him but rather restricts Himself to the righteous influence of His character in wooing them to make their decision. This He has accomplished through the giving of His Son. "The gift of Christ reveals the Father's heart. It testifies that the thoughts of God toward us are 'thoughts of peace, and not of evil.' Jer. 29:11. It declares that while God's hatred of sin is as strong as death, His love for the sinner is stronger than death" (Ibid., 57). When God sent His Son into our world on His rescue mission, He sent with Him all "the riches of the universe" and "the resources of infinite power" and instructed Him to "use these gifts to convince him [man] that *there is no love greater than Mine* in earth or heaven" (Ibid., italics supplied).

By such means it will forever be established that He is indeed the God of the golden rule. God purposes that as we study the life of His Son, we will detect Satan's perversions concerning His character and will finally realize that our greatest happiness is found in loving Him. Thus human beings, angels, and all other inhabitants of the universe will be eternally reconciled to God's rule, and the divine kingdom will forever be placed on a secure platform. The affliction of sin will never rise up a second time (see Nahum 1:9; also *The Desire of Ages,* 26).

A return to the golden rule

God's eternal purpose of reconciling His creatures is to be realized through the revelation of His own character. By beholding the humiliation of the Son of God and, in contrast, by recognizing our selfish natures, we will be led to the foot of the cross; we will pray in a penitent spirit, "Let this mind be in [me], which was also in Christ Jesus" (see Philippians 2:5). As a result, we will choose to bring our lives back into conformity with golden-rule living.

Yet we must never entertain the thought that we can match the level of golden-rule living that was exhibited in Jesus' earthly life. It is true, however, that by beholding that exhibition we will become changed into that same image. Through looking to Him, we will be able, in varying degrees, to reflect those same selfless principles in our own carnal spheres of existence.

This is the great lesson the Lord is seeking to teach every one of us. "And this is life eternal, that they might know thee the only true God [have a mental conception of God's selfless character and ways], and Jesus Christ, whom thou hast sent" (John 17:3). He "hath given us an understanding, that we may know him that is true" (1 John 5:20). We need to have intimate, three-dimensional pictures drawn upon the screens of our minds that portray the selfless characteristics that make up the One we call God. This was God's purpose for Calvary—to show the universe who He really is and what He is really like.

Often we find these revelations a threat to our own carnal security, and thus we react antagonistically toward them. Such unholy attitudes to change are but symptoms of a deeper disease called "discontent." This human malalady is actually based on disbelief of Christ's credibility as well as upon a confusion regarding our own carnal natures. We vitally need a correct understanding of just what Christ is to us and how He is the only One who can fulfill us. Only He can answer the strange enmity we harbor in our hearts, the feelings even we ourselves don't understand.

Let's give Him an honest chance to be our Savior and let Him change us! No one has ever entered into a serious understanding of who Jesus really is and what He has done for us, and remained unmoved. Beholding Christ and His saving work is a stimulating mental feast that creates an insatiable hunger for righteousness, a righteousness that will hurtle us through the threshold of eternity.

So let's now turn to Calvary and learn the lessons of paternal love that will teach us what God is really like.

SAVING BLOOD

The Son of God goes forth to war, A kingly crown to gain;
His blood-red banner streams afar; Who follows in His train?
Who best can drink His cup of woe, Triumph in His pain,
Who patient bears His cross below – He follows in His train.

The martyr, first whose eagle eye, Could pierce beyond the
grave,
Who saw his Master in the sky, And called on Him to save;
Like Him, with pardon on His tongue, In midst of mortal pain,
He prayed for them that did the wrong: Who follows in His train?

A glorious band, the chosen few, On whom the Spirit came;
Twelve valiant saints, Their hope they knew, And mocked the
cross and flame;
They met the tyrant's brandished steel, The lion's gory mane;
They bowed their necks the stroke to feel; Who follows in their
train?

A noble army, men and boys, The matron and the maid,
Around the Saviour's throne rejoice, In robes of light arrayed;
They climbed the steep ascent of heaven, Through peril, toil,
and pain –
O God, to us may grace be given, To follow in their train.

Reginald Heber

CHAPTER

2

The Two Revelations of Calvary—Part 1

God established His government on what we know, in human terms, as the golden rule. This is the constitution of the heavenly government. The desire to better one's self at the expense of another could not flourish in the selfless environment of heaven. Lucifer had become dissatisfied with his position and sought to gain for himself a more prominent place of importance. Yet he knew God's golden-rule government would not constitutionally allow for such an action. Therefore, in order to justify his rebellion in the eyes of the universe, he had to attack God's law.

The strategy he used was to insinuate the accusation among the angels that God Himself did not abide by His own golden-rule policy. Satan has continued to employ this same tactic in trying to blind the minds of men and women toward God. "Satan has represented God as selfish and oppressive, as claiming all, and giving nothing, as requiring the service of His creatures for His own glory, and *making no sacrifice for their good*" (*The Desire of Ages*, 57, italics supplied).

So Lucifer placed God on trial before the entire universe as being selfish. By his decision to reject God's government and His law, sin's originator boldly challenged the eternal security of the universe and claimed that God was the culprit. God's answer to Satan's charges is found in the cross of Calvary. There God took the witness stand in order to testify before human beings and angels. In doing so, He clearly revealed to this fallen world, and even to worlds unfallen, what He is really like.

A deeper understanding of Calvary's lessons will teach us, as nothing else can, the value that heaven places upon a single soul. It will also reveal just how much we need Christ. Calvary is the lens we must use if we ever want to view the great controversy from God's perspective. If we desire to enter into God's feelings and begin to sense just a little of the pain that the sin problem has caused Him, we must consider Calvary. It is the place where God is made real to us, where He becomes credible in our sight. And once our faith is fully established in the credibility of God's character, it will seal our decision to be faithful to Him and His cause. Heaven's calculated purpose in Jesus going to the Cross was not only to make atonement for sin's debt; it was also designed to reveal God's love.

The cross of Calvary teaches us two great lessons. First, it tells us how much God loves the sinner. Second, it shows us how much He hates sin. Right after Adam and Eve sinned, God Himself foretold what was to happen at Calvary. Speaking to Satan after he had caused mankind's fall in Eden, God said, "I will put emnity between thee and the woman, and between thy seed and her seed; it shall bruise thy head, and thou shalt bruise his heel" (Genesis 3:15). Here, of course, was the prophesied result of Calvary, when the conflict between sin and righteousness should peak. There Satan would have God in his hands to do with as he pleased. But in so doing he would reveal to the universe what he really was—a murderer. As a result, many of God's creatures would ultimately decide against Satan and thus choose to aid God in bringing his regime to an end.

God loves the sinner

As God watched the human race fall into the pit of sin, it tugged at His heartstrings of compassion, love, and pity. The

Bible says it moved Him to action. "For God so loved the world, that he gave his only begotten Son" (John 3:16). "The Word was made flesh, and dwelt among us" (John 1:14).

There is much debate today in our church regarding this subject of Christ's incarnation. Exactly what kind of human nature did our Lord take when He came into this world? The nature of Adam *before* he fell or *after* he fell? I'm afraid that in all this argument, we are missing the most important lesson God is trying to teach us in this grand and wonderful subject. When we think about it, we realize that it matters not so much that we be able to define Christ's humanity minutely as it does that we understand the infinite risk He took by becoming human (see *Signs of the Times,* 5 January 1915). This is the lesson heaven is trying to use to change our rebellious attitudes toward God. Yes, God loved the sinner so much that in the person of Jesus He came to "meet life's peril in common with every human soul, to fight the battle as every child of humanity must fight it, *at the risk of failure and eternal loss*" (*The Desire of Ages,* 49, emphasis supplied).

James tells us that "God cannot be tempted with evil" (1:13). When Lucifer broke out in sinful rebellion, he could tempt angels and human beings. But it was literally impossible for him to tempt the Creator. Yet, in order to save fallen humanity, God made a decision to become a creature Himself. He took an infinite risk in that *for the first time God actually placed Himself in a position whereby He could be tempted to sin.*

Evangelical and Catholic theologies maintain that it was impossible for Christ to have sinned while in humanity. But Adventism has never agreed to this. "Many claim that it was impossible for Christ to be overcome by temptation. Then He could not have been placed in Adam's position; He could not have gained the victory that Adam failed to gain. . . . He took the nature of man, with the possibility of yielding to temptation" (*The Desire of Ages,* 117). Out of love for us, our Lord became a human and placed Himself within the firing range of the devil. He actually ran the risk of falling into sin as did Adam! Incarnated, He was truly in our place as the golden rule required. This vaporized Satan's claim that the Godhead was arbitrary and aloof from His created beings.

Even if we don't understand this truth, we can be sure the devil did. Notice his reaction to the news that Jesus would condescend to fight him in the form of a creature. "Satan again rejoiced with his angels that he could, by causing man's fall, pull down the Son of God from His exalted position. He told the angels that when Jesus should take fallen man's nature, he could overpower Him and hinder the accomplishment of the plan of salvation" (*Early Writings*, 152). The degree to which we comprehend this issue will be the degree to which we finally come to love, appreciate, and trust our heavenly Father.

Satan had said God was selfish. He pictured Him as One who just sat upon His throne and lived off the nectar of His creatures' service. But in giving His eternal Son to the human race, God put all of heaven, the entire universe, and even His own eternal throne on the bargaining table. This is what Ellen White was trying to tell us way back in 1895. She said, "Remember that Christ risked all; 'tempted like as we are,' he *staked even his own eternal existence* upon the issue of the conflict. *Heaven itself was imperiled for our redemption.* At the foot of the cross, remembering that for *one sinner* Jesus would have yielded up his life, we may *estimate the value of a soul*" (*General Conference Bulletin*, 1 December 1895).

Although we have difficulty comprehending it, God considers each one of us more valuable than His own eternal existence. Like the widow who was willing to yield her two mites, our God was willing to give up everything He possessed for us. If we will just contemplate this truth, Satan's lie that God is selfish will be broken. It will make God believable in our eyes and cause us to affectionately seal our love and appreciation for Him. We will see Him as truly worthy of our worship because only in Him can we find our true self-worth. Then we, too, will join with the other citizens of the universe in proclaiming, "Worthy is the Lamb that was slain to receive power, and riches, and wisdom, and strength, and honour, and glory, and blessing" (Revelation 5:12).

I used to think that if Christ had sinned in His humanity He would simply have gone back to heaven and said something like "I'm sorry Father. I tried My best to save the human race, but I just wasn't able to do it." But I've come to understand that greater issues were at stake in the conflict. Had Christ sinned, then He, one of the eternal members of the divine Godhead, would have switched allegiance and would have been working "at cross purposes with God"(see *SDA Bible Commentary,* vol. 5, p. 1082). Simple deduction concludes that the unity of the Godhead would have been split up. The very unity that our Savior had with His Father, and which He most earnestly prayed in John 17 that we might also have with Them, would have been eternally severed. A divine member of the eternal Godhead would have become subject to sin, thus providing the kingdom of darkness access to divine power.

Some may be tempted to think that God didn't really take such a risk, because He could see from the beginning to the end of the whole ordeal. Surely He knew from the onset that Christ wasn't going to yield to Satan's temptations. But this fact does not change the genuineness of the risk. God also knew beforehand that angels and men were going to turn against Him. Yet in spite of such foreknowledge, He still went through with the plan to create them. The deeper lesson to be realized here is that if God had foreknown that Christ would have yielded to evil, thus bringing eternal conseqences upon the universe, He would still have chosen to go through with the plan! When it came to the sin issue, it was all or nothing with God. Christ sacrificed everything for man in order to make it possible for him to gain heaven. If sin, when given an equal opportunity, could prove itself more powerful than righteousness, then it deserved to be the ruling force in the cosmos. But if righteousness prevailed, then sin had no legitimate reason to exist.

What's more, if God had simply challenged sin with no real risk involved, no doubt Satan would have cried "Foul play" to the universe. The devil would have never consented to fight a pretend battle in which he had no real chance of winning. No, No! The devil full well understood that there was a real risk involved. This was his once-in-a-lifetime opportunity to fulfill his desire to become like God. The stakes were high for Satan, as well as for Christ. If Satan won, he would defeat Christ before the universe. But if he lost, his whole cause would be lost, and his doom would be sure.

No wonder the angels in heaven and the inhabitants of the unfallen worlds anxiously held their breath during those thirty some odd years that Jesus walked our earth. They knew that Satan was tempting not just a mere man but God. They knew that if Jesus had chosen to yield to temptation, as did Adam, the very power of God would have come crumbling right down and would have fallen into Satan's lap. They realized that not only the salvation of mankind but the security of the heavenly universe and their own eternal destiny, as well, was hanging in the balance as Jesus battled Satan in humanity.

But the most incredible part of all this is yet to come. How many of us sinful human beings would have to accept the rescue Jesus offered before God would be willing to risk the security of His throne, heaven, and the unfallen worlds? The answer to this question is what will finally break our antagonistic hearts and cause us to fall eternally in love with God. *He would have done it for just one of us, no matter who we are or how bad we have been.*

The Bible lesson of the good shepherd and his ninety-nine sheep teaches that our great Shepherd, Jesus Christ, would leave the entire flock while venturing to save just one lost sheep. Incredible thought! God would have made the decision to put the entire universe at risk, and even His own throne, in an attempt to save any *one* of us. In His estimation, one helpless human enslaved by sin was—and still is—as valuable as a whole universe that has never sinned. This is how much God loves you and me even if we are still sinners. Remember, "while we were yet sinners, Christ died for us" (Romans 5:8).

Oh, if we could only grasp what is at stake in this great controversy. When we finally comprehend that God has an eternal investment in each of us, it will disarm us and cause us to lay down our selfish defenses against the Holy Spirit. It will convince us that God is genuinely interested and involved in our personal lives. May it result in a response that causes our hands to grow limp around the coveted treasure of sin. May we reach out and grab the offered Gift, Jesus Christ, and hold on to Him as we would hold to a lifeboat in a stormy sea. May His undimmed ardor that drove Him to pay so much, most of which we can't even comprehend, be rewarded by our returned love and loyalty.

When this truth finally hits home to our hearts, it will cause us to take notice of what He has been trying to tell us since ages past through His prophets. Then we will render implicit obedience to whatever He requires because we will finally be convinced that He really does have our best interest at heart. We will then see that He is someone we can truly believe in because He has shown Himself to be true to us, as displayed in the Incarnation. We will realize that He is forever on our side. And you can be sure that this truth is what Satan is so determined that we never understand. He knows it is the very knowledge that will influence us to put on "the whole armour of God" (Ephesians 6:13) and seal our decision against him.

I gave My life for thee, My precious blood I shed,
That thou might'st ransomed be, and quickened from the dead.
I gave, I gave My life for thee, What hast thou given for Me?
I gave, I gave My life for thee, What hast thou given for Me?

SAVING BLOOD

My Father's house of light, My glory circled throne,
I left for earthly night, For wanderings sad and lone;
I left, I left it all for thee, Hast thou left aught for Me?
I left, I left it all for thee, Hast thou left aught for Me?

I suffered much for thee, More than thy tongue can tell,
Of bitterest agony, To rescue thee from hell;
I've borne, I've borne it all for thee, What hast thou borne for
Me?
I've borne, I've borne it all for thee, What hast thou borne for
Me?

Frances Ridley Havergal

CHAPTER 3

The Two Revelations of Calvary—Part 2

In our last chapter we discovered that Calvary not only teaches us how much God loves the sinner but also how much He hates sin. Satan tries to distort our understanding of God's character in this area, as he does in others. As we discover that God is love, Satan tries to lead us into an extreme view of that love.

Christians everywhere go and tell those who are openly involved in sin that God loves them. Of course, it is true; God *does* love the willful sinner. But we must be careful when proclaiming this fact not to imply that His love is synonymous with salvation. Christ is not "the minister of sin" (Galatians 2:17). If God's love is not laid out clearly in all its aspects, the devil will lead people to believe that because God loves them so much He won't destroy them even if they continue in their sinful ways. "Satan deceives many with the plausible theory that God's love for His people is so great that He will excuse sin in them; he represents that while the threatenings of God's word are to serve a certain purpose in His moral government, they are never to be literally fulfilled" (*Patriarchs and Prophets*, 522).

The final result of sin is to bring eternal oblivion upon the universe and its inhabitants. From it's very inception, that is where sin has been leading. So, on the cross Christ went through the experience of passing into that oblivion, with no hope of a resurrection. He who knew no sin became sin for us. He actually experienced the eternal separation of the unity He had with His Father, just as He would have experienced had He chosen to sin (see *The Desire of Ages*, 687, 753). This is why on the cross He cried out in agony, " 'My God, my God, why hast thou forsaken me?' " (Mark 15:34). Here we see the agony that God the Son was going through while being separated from His Father. But what about the Father? What was going on in heaven as it witnessed God sacrificing His divine Lamb?

A farmer went out one day with his eight-year-old son to do some mowing with his tractor. As he was driving along, he felt the machinery behind him roughly run over something. Turning to look, he saw that his son had fallen from the tractor's fender where he had been sitting. Then the reality hit him that he had just run over his only little boy with the destructive blades. Stopping the tractor, he quickly got off and ran back to the place where the ground was now strewn with debris and blood. For a moment he seemed to be in a dream. Then reality quickly told him that this was no dream; it was a living nightmare! The poor father fell to the ground, clutching the dirt and wailing in agony, "My God, my God, what have I done! I've killed my boy! I've killed my boy!" That is a true story.

Such is only a faint reflection of what the Godhead went through as they witnessed the scenes of Calvary. We must understand that although we experience things in our finite realm, God lives in an infinite realm, and everything He experiences is infinitely intensified. We are told that "when the Father beheld the sacrifice of His Son, He bowed before it in recognition of it's perfection. 'It is enough,' He said, 'the atonement [in the sense of payment for sin's debt] is complete' " (*Review and Herald*, 24 September 1901). We can be sure, however, that it was in no casual sense that the Father got down off His throne and cried

"It is enough!" Calvary caused Him to come stumbling off His throne, like the father came stumbling off that tractor, and with a cry that sent shock waves powerful enough to cause this planet itself to quake, God proclaimed, "It is enough! It is enough! I can't take it anymore!" Just as David cried when he learned of the death of his son Absalom, " 'O my son Absalom, my son, my son Absalom! would God I had died for thee, O Absalom, my son, my son!' " (2 Samuel 18:33).

Inspiration tells us that the "interruption of the communion between God and His Son caused a condition of things in the heavenly courts which cannot be described by human language" (*SDA Bible* Commentary, 5:1108). Heaven was silenced as it beheld the awful agony of God. Oh, when are we going to realize that God is a personal being? He has feelings and emotions just as you and I do. Yet we often come to church week after week and worship Him as if He were a god made of unfeeling substance such as wood or stone. It is His desire, and our privilege, for us to understand and appreciate Him for who He is and what He is like (see Acts 17:29).

The problem is that we are numb to the serious reality of the great-controversy issues. It is much more comfortable for us humans to get caught up in a movie or a ballgame—anything that will relieve our minds from contemplating the seriousness of the consequences that sin brings to our lives. This is why comedians stay in so much demand while the church pews remain empty. Like the disciples in Gethsemane, we say, "Let us sleep, Lord, and wake us up when it is all over." But true religion inevitably brings us face to face with the reality of what is going on between us and God, just as it did for Abraham when he was called upon to sacrifice his son Isaac. The bitter and sorrowful experiences of this life are intended to help us gain a better understanding of what the aching heart of our compassionate God is feeling.

But why did God have to go through this experience of beholding the agony of His divine Son? Because through His Son

He consented "to be sin for us," although He "knew no sin" (2 Corinthians 5:21). As a result, He now has the legal right to declare all who are unrighteousness to be as righteous as He is Himself (see Philippians 3:9). Even though He was perfectly innocent of sin, out of love for us and by His own choice He decided to suffer the eternal consequences of our sins by dying "the death of the cross" (Philippians 2:8). Thus, in His own experience, Christ brought sin's consequences to their full fruition—the breakup of the unity of the Godhead. This is why He now has every right to wipe sin out of existence. "For this purpose the Son of God was manifested, that he might destroy the works of the devil [sin]" (1 John 3:8; see also Hebrews 2:14).

The Bible plainly tells us that God Himself will one day destroy this sinful world, along with those sinners who willfully choose its ways (see 2 Peter 3:1-14). However, we must be careful how we ourselves perceive God's destructive act and how we present it to others, or God will surely be misrepresented. In the game of cops and robbers, our natural sympathies often end up with the robbers, while the cops, who try to maintain law and order, get the bad press. God forbid that we should put our gracious Lord in the "cop" image, yet He does police the universe with eternal vigilance to protect the innocent.

Where we often get confused is in trying to make God's personality synonomous with His enforcement of divine justice. We read about God's destructive wrath and automatically try to equate that with His character. God does not maintain universal justice because He enjoys doing so but, rather, because He *has to* in order to provide for the safety and peace of the universe. It is what the law requires in order that there be liberty and justice for all. This is why God's law is called the "law of liberty" (James 2:12).

"It is in mercy to the universe that God will finally destroy the rejecters of His grace" (*The Great Controversy*, 543). Whenever and wherever sin is threatening the eternal security of His people, God takes action against it. In light of God's intense desire to save, one can better understand why the Bible calls the destruction of sin and sinners His "strange act" (Isaiah 28:21).

So, it will be at the end when sin and sinners are destroyed in the lake of fire. As the wicked marshal their forces around the walls of the golden city of God, their plan of attack will be to storm the city and take it captive. It's hard to imagine that anyone would presume to do such a thing, but such is the level of self-deception at this time. As they march toward the city, the wicked will be shown what they have given up. They will also be brought to a painful recognition of the results of their willful course to others and to God. The fact that they will now reap what they have sown will be vividly brought before their minds. Though they may bow and proclaim God to be just, there is no real repentance in their utterances. They are not capable of repenting, so often they have refused it before. For them, to continue to exist with this knowledge of their lost state would be misery beyond expression.

Next to Calvary, this last confrontation between good and evil will be the most excruciating scene the universe has ever had to witness. There on that plain the infection of both fallen humanity and fallen angels will reach its crisis. All creation will be groaning, like a woman in labor waiting to be delivered, as God prepares to usher in eternal bliss.

I have always thought of the destruction of the wicked as an event in which God takes the initiative. But during this time, both the righteous and the unrighteous will be crying out for God to end the miserable situation. So it is that God, acting as both a Protector of the righteous and a merciful Father toward His children who are lost, will do what only a merciful and just God must do. "And fire came down from God out of heaven, and devoured them" (Revelation 20:9).

God is forced to intervene and save His people by annihilating sin in the persons of the wicked. But God will take no pleasure in their destruction (see Ezekiel 33:11). Sin will once again place Him in that agonizing situation that caused Him to weep in agony outside of Jerusalem, like the father wept over his boy whom he had accidentally killed. There, while overlooking that doomed city, Christ's "eyes fill[ed] with tears, and His body rock[ed] to and fro like a tree before the tempest, while a wail of anguish burst . . . from His quivering lips, as if from the depths of a broken heart. . . . Israel's King was in tears; not silent tears of gladness, but tears and groans of insuppressible agony" (*The Desire of Ages*, 575, 576). As we behold this scene of God suffering over His lost creation at the lake of fire, we shall better understand. As we picture Him in the dirt, clutching the grass as it were, with groanings pouring forth from His soul that will be powerful enough to send shock waves throughout all creation, we will be, no doubt, like those standing with Him outside Jerusalem who "wept in sympathy with a grief they could not comprehend" (Ibid.). Then we will all have a fuller realization that God did everything He could to separate the perishing sinners from their sins, but they refused. They loved their sins more than they loved God and what was right.

When God makes a final end of sin and sinners, it will be necessary that He does a thorough job. Often when we approach someone who is involved in sin and try to counsel him or her, that person becomes defensive and tells us that what he does with his life is his own business. But such people simply do not understand the nature of sin. It is a scientific fact that a single body cell that becomes infected with the AIDS (HIV) virus has the potential to ultimately bring about the destruction of the entire body. Likewise, it is a known fact among the unfallen citizens of the universe that just one creature who willfully cherishes sin, even in the remotest part of the universe, endangers the entire creation because he has within himself the capacity to bring about its complete destruction. We must never forget that the sin problem that has wrecked our little world and caused every inhabitant throughout the universe to shudder, had its beginning in the heart of a single creature, the angel Lucifer. And before the universe can ever be free from the dangers that sin poses, not one unrepentant sinner can be left in existence.

Concerning the time when this eradication of sin is accomplished, note this description: "The great controversy is ended. Sin and sinners are no more. *The entire universe is clean*. One pulse of harmony and gladness beats through the vast creation. . . . From the minutest atom to the greatest world, all things, animate and inanimate, in their unshadowed beauty and perfect joy, declare that God is love" (*The Great Controversy*, 678). Though we may not understand it all now, we can, by faith, rest assured that whatever God does He will do with our best interest in mind. Our heavenly Father so desires our happiness that once the great controversy is over He will wipe away any remembrance we have of the pain that sin brought to us and our loved ones. Speaking of that time, He says, "the former troubles are forgotten. . . For, behold, I create new heavens and a new earth: and the former shall not be remembered, nor come into mind. . . weeping shall be no more heard" (Isaiah 65:16-19; see also verses 20-25).

But it will not be so with God. The eternal scars He bears on His body are but representative of the scars He will bear in His memory. Throughout eternity His great heart of love and compassion will be aching for His beloved creatures who chose to rebel against Him.

Considering all this, should we not actually be feeling sorry for God? Isn't it a tragedy that He is being forced into a situation in which some day He must, of necessity, put an end to the existence of multitudes of His children whom He created, loves, and for whom He even gave His own eternal life? It would be as if we had to kill and destroy our own children. As we come to understand such things more clearly, it will melt our hard hearts, and we will actually weep for God just as the prophet said we would (see Zechariah 12:10).

Can we not begin to sense why God hates sin so much? Sin is costly in the eyes of God. "In order to fully realize the value of salvation [from sin], it is necessary to understand what it cost" (*Testimonies for the Church*, 2:200). As we daily contemplate the "infinite risk" and "eternal sacrifice" that was required in order to prevent sin from destroying the universe, our attitude about sin being harmless will change. And so will our willingness to commit it. "He who sees the guilt of his transgression, and understands the infinite sacrifice made in his behalf, will not continue in sin" (*Signs of the Times*, 15 November 1899). "It is when we most fully comprehend the love of God that we best realize the sinfulness of sin. When we see the length of the chain that was let down for us, when we understand something of the infinite sacrifice that Christ has made in our behalf, the heart is melted with tenderness and contrition" (*Steps to Christ*, 36).

This is the great truth that is to arouse the church here in the end time and motivate her to fulfill the gospel commission. "The last message of mercy to be given to the world, is a revelation of His [God's] character of love" (*Christ's Object Lessons*, 415). This message of Christ's self-sacrificing love will soon reach clear around the globe. When the church contemplates that love to the point that we are transformed into a reflective image of it, we will receive the seal of God, share the knowledge of His infinite love with the entire world, and then be translated.

That's the way it was with Enoch, whose experience was a type for God's final generation of saints. "The infinite, unfathomable love of God through Christ became the subject of his [Enoch's] meditations day and night. With all the fervor of his soul he sought to reveal that love to the people among whom he dwelt" (*Testimonies to the Church*, 8:329). That infinite, unfathomable love can be understood only through contemplating the infinite, unfathomable risk.

It will be in the framework of God's magnificent character

of love, as revealed through His infinite sacrifice, that the remnant church will finally be aroused to give the loud cry to a world perishing in sin. "When we begin to comprehend what a sacrifice Christ made in order to save a perishing world, there will be seen a mighty wrestling to save souls. Oh, that all our churches might see and realize the infinite sacrifice of Christ!" (*Testimonies for the Church*, 9:125, 126). Surely this will indeed be the centerpiece of that angel's message by whose glory "the earth was lightened" (Revelation 18:1).

I hear the Savior say, "Thy strength indeed is small;
Child of weakness, watch and pray, Find in Me thine all in all."
Lord, now indeed I find Thy power, and Thine alone,
Can change the leper's spots, And melt the heart of stone.
Since nothing good have I Whereby Thy grace to claim,
I'll wash my garment white In the blood of Calvary's Lamb.
And when before The throne I stand in Him complete,
I'll lay my trophies down, All down at Jesus' feet.
Jesus paid it all, All to Him I owe;
Sin had left a crimson stain; He washed it white as snow.

—Elvina M. Hall

CHAPTER

4

One-on-One
With God

"We never knew raising children to love and serve God was going to be such a challenge." Such was the testimony shared by John and Debbie Thompson at a group study on Christian parenting. They thought it was an easy task, even fun, when their three children—Sheila, Ray, and Sandy—were little. But their confession resulted from a miscalculation as to what would happen as the children got older and began to think for themselves.

Understandably, John and Debbie were concerned for their children's eternal welfare. Some considered the Thompson home a "strict environment." No doubt this was due to the fact that the Thompson's had laid down some unbendable rules in an attempt to govern the family's conduct. In their younger years, the children never thought to question the "whys" and "why nots" of the family's regulations. Their interests seemed to be riveted on such things as Mom's apple pies, playing in the treehouse, and taking nature walks on Sabbath.

But as the children grew and their minds began to mature, almost automatically they began to wonder "why" and "why not." All of a sudden the family rules became the object of intense discussion in the Thompson home. It was then that John and Debbie found themselves confronted with challenges they had never before considered. Sixteen-year-old Ray now wanted to know why he wasn't allowed to take the family car and go out on a date without a chaperone like his friend Jerry was able to do. The girls were having a difficult time understanding what was really so bad about lipstick and simple jewelry. After all, most of the other kids at school were into it.

For John and Debbie, it all seemed like a mountain that had no peak. The dawning of each day introduced new and perplexing confrontations. To them, it seemed ironic that they were the ones now telling parents with younger children, "Just wait till your children get older." But John and Debbie were simply advancing in their studies at the University of Jesus.

You see, God in His mercy allows us to pass through varied experiences down here in order that we might, to some degree, identify with what He is dealing with on a much larger scale. As we observe and participate in the administration of the governments of homes, churches, and nations here below, we learn vital lessons about how God's universal government functions. To learn to lead subjects into a willing submission to what is right, without the use of force, is to learn the science of salvation. It is what constitutes true education.

God's method of education, whether in the home or classroom, leads the learner to understand the great principles by which His government operates. By precept and example, parents and teachers are to teach their subjects lessons of moral responsibility, personal accountability, and self government. They are "to train the youth to be thinkers, and not mere reflectors of other men's thoughts" (*Education*, 17). And this is exactly what God is trying to teach each of us in His school—how to think and choose for ourselves, as well as being willing to bear responsibility for the choices we make.

Always blaming God

In a way, what went on in the Thompson's family government is what has happened in God's government. Many of their friends felt that the reason the Thompson children were rebelling was that the family rules were too rigid. At least that was what the children were insinuating. Thus it was made to appear that John and Debbie were the cause of all the insurrection because of their "strict standards."

This is exactly what Lucifer claimed to be the cause of sin. "Lucifer took the position that as a result of the law of God, wrong existed in heaven and on this earth. This brought against God's government the charge of being arbitrary. But this is a falsehood, framed by the author of all falsehoods. God's government is a government of free-will, and there is no act of rebellion or obedience which is not an act of free-will" (*Signs of the Times*, 5 June 1901). From the onset of the great controversy, the fairness of God's government has been called into question. Yet all the while God has maintained to all the inhabitants of the universe that His "is a government of personal responsibility" (*Signs of the Times*, July 11, 1900). In other words, God has been saying that in no way is He responsible for the sin that has manifested itself among His creatures. Rather, each individual is responsible for his or her own sin. Sin is a result of one's own personal decision to disregard the order that divine wisdom has established.

But the heart that is in rebellion against God and His law refuses to admit this. It seeks to blame anything and everyone in an attempt to avoid confessing its own personal accountability for the sin problem. However, to blame circumstances and others is to indirectly blame God. The devil blamed God; Eve blamed the devil; Adam blamed Eve; and we all blame Adam. This is all in an attempt to sidestep genuine repentance and to justify self. "The inquiry of many a proud heart is, 'Why need I go in penitence and humiliation before I can have the assurance of my acceptance with God' " (*Steps to Christ*, 45). But God speaks to us through inspiration and says, "True repentance will lead a man to bear his guilt himself and acknowledge it without deception or hypocrisy. . . . Those who do acknowledge their guilt will be justified. . . . Genuine repentance and humiliation reveal a spirit of confession in which there is no excuse for sin or attempt at self-justification" (Ibid., 40, 41).

Without question, the natural heart has a difficult time accepting its own personal responsibility for sin. We look at the world around us and question how it is that evil is allowed to exist under the sovereignty of God. We read the biblical account of Adam's fall and the entrance of sin into our world and say, "It's not my fault that Adam sinned. How can God be fair in holding me accountable for something I didn't even have a choice in?"

It is vitally important that we sort these things out. To begin with, God does not hold us personally or legally accountable for Adam's fatal decision to sin. One could not find a civilized earthly government that would hold children responsible for the misconduct of their parents. If God did that, then He would be arbitrary, as Satan has charged. Every child born since Adam would have a valid argument in the judgment to question God's fairness.

Through the Bible, God has plainly revealed His thoughts in this matter. He says, "The fathers shall not be put to death for the children, neither shall the children be put to death for the fathers: every man shall be put to death for his own sin" (Deuteronomy 24:16). "The son shall not bear the iniquity of the father, neither shall the father bear the iniquity of the son" (Ezekiel 18:20).

But though God does not personally condemn us for our forefather's sins, we naturally bear the consequences of their wrong actions. This consequential catastrophe dates all the way back to Adam's sin. Romans 5 makes it clear that our first father's transgression opened the door for sin and death to be passed on to every one of us.

But that death does not include condemnation to *eternal* death. According to God's justice system, a person is never condemned for sin unless he knowingly breaks the law. "Justice requires that man shall have light" (*Signs of the Times*, 27 May 1902), and "condemnation only follows the rejection of light" (*Testimonies for the Church*, 2:286). "The children were not condemned for the sins of the parents; but when, with a knowledge of all the light given to their parents, the children rejected the additional light granted to themselves, they became partakers of the parents' sins, and filled up the measure of their iniquity" (*The Great Controversy*, 28). "They will not be condemned because they do not know the way, the truth, and the life. The truth that has reached their understanding, the light which has shone on the soul, but which has been neglected or refused, will condemn them. Those who never had the light to reject will not be in condemnation" (*Testimonies for the Church*, 2:123).

The Lord Himself taught this lesson. "If I had not come and spoken unto them, they had not had sin: but now they have no cloke for their sin" (John 15:22). In commenting on this verse, Ellen White added, "There is no condemnation where light is not given" (*Signs of the Times*, 22 November 1885). These truths about God's fairness are plain.

"But," someone says, "what about where the Bible says, 'Visiting the iniquity of the fathers upon the children unto the third and fourth generation of them that hate Me' "? (see Exodus 20: 5). Ellen White clarifies that this verse is speaking about the *consequences* of the parents sin, not punishment for them. "It is inevitable that children should suffer from the consequences of parental wrongdoing, but they are not punished for the parents' guilt, except as they participate in their sins" (*Patriarchs and Prophets*, 306).

Throughout the Bible there are stories, such as that of Achan, where the innocent bear the consequences of another person's choice to sin. But that does not mean that God arbitrarily condemned the innocent for another's crime. In practical terms, one may receive from his father a disposition to alcoholism, but it would not be fair to hold him personally accountable for all of his father's drunken revelings. Likewise, an innocent victim may be killed as a consequence of another person's decision to drink and drive, but though a victim of circumstances, he does not share in the guilt of the crime.

Born to die?

If the death we received from Adam does not include condemnation for Adam's sin, then why do we have to die? It is imperative that we make a clear distinction here between the first and second death.

The first death is the one that we receive from Adam. Ellen White brings this fact out clearly in her book, *The Great Controversy*. " 'The wages of sin is *death*; but the gift of God is eternal life through Jesus Christ our Lord.' Romans 6:23. . . . Moses declared to Israel: 'I have set before thee this day life and good, and *death* and evil.' Deuteronomy 30:15. The death referred to in these scriptures *is not that pronounced upon Adam*, for all mankind suffer the penalty of his transgression. *It is 'the second death'* that is placed in contrast with everlasting life" (544, emphasis supplied).

In addition to this "first death," that is the natural consequence of sin, Adam also equipped each of us with what it takes to commit eternal suicide ourselves—a carnal nature that is inclined to disobey. This is why the Bible states that "by nature [we are] the children of wrath" (Ephesians 2:3). Notice that it says we are subject to wrath "by nature" and not "by Adam." If left to run its course, our nature will inevitably lead us to commit a "sin unto death," the second death (see 1 John 5:16, 17). Yet this second death results from our own decision to follow Adam's example of disobedience. Only by putting a check on that corrupt nature, by choosing the second birth, can we escape the second death.

To help clarify this point, consider this example. Suppose

that a child is born to a mother who passes on to him a fatal disease through heredity. It is a disease that most likely will not allow him to live to see his twentieth birthday. This young man becomes bitter toward his mother for having passed on to him this life-threatening condition. He complains that he never asked to be born to this woman and certainly never asked to inherit her problems. He is a victim of his mother's genetic disorder. However, when the young man turns sixteen, he hears the good news that medical science has discovered a cure for his disease. Yet he refuses to get the available help. Now suppose that when he is nineteen, he is admitted to the hospital and given only a few days to live. We pay him a visit and discover that he is still extremely bitter toward his mother for the predicament in which she has placed him. He continues to blame her for the fact that he is going to die, even though he has himself rejected available help. Who, now, is responsible for his death—the boy or his mother?

It is not an arbitrary divine pronouncement that condemns us. That would be to say that God had a choice in our becoming sinners. He simply knew the inevitable results of the nature we inherited. He knows we will all choose on our own to "go astray" (see Isaiah 53:6). So He concluded us "all under sin" (Galatians 3:22). He gathered in one lump sum all the individual choices to sin by Adam's descendants. Then He Himself bore the collective consequences of those decisions—the guilt and condemnation—on Calvary's cross. We must understand that He concluded us all under sin not for the purpose of condemning us. Instead, He did so in order to be able to justifiably extend His mercy to the entire human race, even to those yet unborn. "For God hath concluded them all in unbelief, that he might have mercy upon all" (Romans 11:32). But if we reject the antidote of Christ's saving blood, then like the boy in our example, we become personally accountable for our own fate.

God has allowed all of us to become subject to the first death.

This direct consequence of Adam's sin is an object lesson intended to deter us from going to the grave in disobedience. The experience of watching loved ones die teaches us the reality of sin's consequences. Without controversy, funerals are among the most solemn events in which humans participate. They are calculated to inspire in us a desire to cooperate with God's plan to save, to lead us away from choosing the second death.

Jesus doesn't want us to worry unduly about the first death, the death we received from Adam, because He can rectify that. In fact, He proved it by raising Lazarus from the dead. But if we reject the light of truth given to us in this lifetime, it will result in the second death, and there will be nothing that even God Himself can do to reverse that decision on our part or its consequences. "The soul that sinneth [chooses, individually, to sin], it shall die" (Ezekiel 18:20).

One of the primary reasons people reject this idea of personal accountability and lean instead toward corporate condemnation is the issue of the fate of infants. They reason that if it takes a willful choice to incur the second death, then babies don't need a Savior, since they haven't willfully chosen to sin. The question of what happens to babies and children who die before reaching the age of accountability has sparked many a debate among Christians for centuries. In the Catholic religion, such study led to the doctrine of infant baptism. Though we Adventists reject such a teaching, we, too, have developed among us a myriad of theories as to just how God is going to deal with such cases.

But the Bible does not give us sufficient light on what happens to those who do not qualify as accountable beings—infants, the mentally retarded, etc. The gospel, as far as we can safely understand it, deals only with beings whom God considers accountable. Regarding such questions as what will happen to babies who die, we would no doubt do well to heed Ellen White's counsel.

Whether all the children of unbelieving parents will be saved we cannot tell, because God has not made known His purpose in regard to this matter, and we had better leave it where God has left it and dwell upon subjects made plain in His Word. . . .This we should consider as one of the questions we are not at liberty to express a position or an opinion upon, for the simple reason that God has not told us definitely about this matter in His Word. If He thought it was essential for us to know, He would have plainly told us. . . . There are things we do not now understand (*Selected Messages*, 3:313-315).

Obviously this is a matter we must be content to let rest in the hands of God. We need to trust that He will be fair and that He will do what He knows to be best in each case. Any suggestion regarding the fate of such cases is only speculation at best. And it is certainly unwise to frame a system of theology on human opinions based on speculation.

It suits the devil's purposes quite well to convince us of a corporate view of the gospel. To think that God holds me responsible for the sin of someone else is to destroy individual accountability—although I may certainly suffer the consequences of their sinful choices. A corporate view of sin and the gospel says that I, as an individual, don't count. It suggests that I'm just a spectator, yes, even a pawn, in a cosmic game of chess, being positioned on the board by someone else's decision. Such theological views tend to negate the one-on-one relationship that God is seeking to establish with each soul.

Chief of sinners though I be, Jesus shed His blood for me;
Died that I might live on high, Died that I might never die;
As the branch is to the vine, I am His, and He is mine.

One-on-One With God

O the height of Jesus' love! Higher than the heaven above,
Deeper than the deepest sea, Lasting as eternity;
Love that found me – wondrous thought! Found me when I
sought Him not!

Chief of sinners though I be, Christ is all in all to me;
All my wants to Him are known, All my sorrows are His own;
Safe with Him from earthly strife, He sustains the hidden life.

William McComb

CHAPTER
5

Light, Faith, and Choice

It was New Year's Eve 1998. I decided to make a quick stop at the local supermarket on my way home before spending the evening with family and friends. But the stop turned out to be anything but quick!

A winter blizzard was forecast for later that evening, and the store was a mass of people frantically scurrying up and down the aisles, emptying shelves as they went. The checkout lanes were backed up like a rush-hour Chicago freeway; baskets were loaded down with nearly every food item imaginable.

In an attempt to curb my growing impatience, I picked up a copy of *LIFE* magazine featuring the year's review in pictures. While thumbing through photos of Bill and Hillary Clinton, Ken Starr and Monica Lewinsky, Mark McGuire and the other human images that were indelibly impressed upon our memories during that year, I saw it. It was one of those haunting scenes that cause you to lie awake at night and think. It was a picture of a famished mother standing against a wall in Sudan, while her starving three-year-old child crawled across the ground in front of her. The child's bones were protruding in every direction; his stomach swollen like a helium balloon. A look of total despair and hopelessness filled his cavernous eyes—a true snapshot of humanity that had given up the battle for survival.

Suddenly, the stark reality that more than 40,000 people die of starvation every day in our world came crashing down around my Americanized senses. I immediately lost my appetite and felt like fleeing the scene of that overcrowded food store. It is in such moments that even the most earnest Christian pauses to wonder, "Where is God in humanity's time of need? Is He there? Does He care?"

Squarely and Fairly

If we just go by what we see, the conclusion would seem to be that Satan is winning the continuing battle for souls. It often appears that God is standing back and allowing multitudes to be deceived and destroyed by the devil, with no saving knowledge of Him. Yet this is not how the universe views it. And the Bible tells us that we also need to look not "at the things which are seen, but at the things which are not seen" (2 Corinthians 4:18). The eye of faith reveals that God is dealing squarely and fairly with every single creature.

To us, it may appear unfair that we receive the consequences of a carnal nature and a fallen environment. But the Lord makes up for these degenerate conditions with compensating factors of light, faith, and choice. The Bible tells us that Christ "lighteth every man that cometh into the world" (John 1:9) and has given to everyone a "measure of faith" (Romans 12:3). These spiritual tools, coupled with the free will to utilize them, is all that accountable beings need in order to obtain eternal life.

One thing is certain: Everyone who is saved in the end will be saved through Christ's saving blood. Since Jesus is the " 'light of the world' " (John 8:12), any degree of saving light that a person receives is from Him. Though the degree of understanding that is enlightened be miniscule, if a person follows that light, he or she is a follower of Christ whether knowingly or unknowingly. Of such Jesus says, " 'I know them, and they follow me: and I give unto them eternal life; and they shall never perish' " (John 10:27, 28).

In an earlier chapter, we saw that God would have risked His own eternal existence in order to save just one soul. He has invested the entire universe in every single person, regardless of who they may be. " 'God is no respecter of persons' " (Acts 10:34). Can we honestly conclude, then, that He is going to allow Satan to destroy human beings by the truckloads for eternity while He just stands by and watches? Are we not of more value to Him than that? Didn't Jesus say that God noticed even the demise of sparrows that were worth only about half a farthing each in the estimation of men? And didn't He teach that we are " 'of more value than many sparrows' " (Matthew 10:31)? We must never lose sight of the fact that God has made an infinite investment in each one of us. And like the stockbroker who daily reads his *Wall Street Journal*, God is so interested in each of our lives that He keeps a running total of how many hairs we have on our head (Matthew 10:30).

"One soul is of infinite value; Calvary speaks its worth" (*Gospel Workers*, 184). It is not surprising, then, to learn that the Savior has a concentrated interest in every person. "The relations between God and each soul are as distinct and full as though there were not another soul upon the earth to share His watchcare, not another soul for whom He gave His beloved Son" (*Steps to Christ*, 100).

It was this understanding of a personal God that caused such individuals as Mary Magdalene, Bartimaeus, and the demoniacs of Gadara to make a full surrender to Christ. The knowledge finally dawned upon their darkened minds that God cared for them personally. Jesus was not just the Savior of the world; He was their personal Savior. By discerning His love for them, their love for Him was awakened. The concept of God's goodness toward them personally entered into their experience and led them to repentance. And it is this same revelation of God's personal love that is going to melt the hard-heartedness of our generation. There is a saying that's true—"Believing that Christ died is history, but believing that He died *for you* is salvation."

Though it often appears that Satan is deceiving many honest souls, this is far from the truth. Such thoughts paint a terrible picture of God's watchcare over the creatures for whom He died. It presumes that God is going to allow someone to be lost because a sufficient amount of saving light never came to them.

In the parable of the rich man and Lazarus, this is the same complaint the rich man lodged against God. In fact, Christ sought to counteract such false assumptions by telling that parable. The lesson to be gathered from it is that every man is given sufficient light for the discharge of the duties required of him. (see *Christ's Object Lessons*, 264, 265).

The Holy Spirit is constantly at work in the cities and in the countryside, on the land and on the sea. Wherever human beings are found, divine agencies are dispatched as ministering spirits, bringing to all some degree of saving light. If this light is conscientiously followed, however little it may be, it will yield its possessor eternal life. The second chapter of Romans reveals that even those among the rawest of heathen cultures are not overlooked by the saving eye of grace (see *The Desire of Ages*, 638, 639; Romans 2:14-16). Many will be saved who never were fully enlightened about the gospel in this life and who will need to have it explained to them when they are resurrected.

Though we may indeed influence others for or against God, the Lord has arranged it so that if anyone is lost it will ultimately be because of his or her own decision. If a single soul could be eternally lost because that person didn't have sufficient saving light bestowed upon him, then that soul would have a valid objection to God's fairness, one that could not be overruled in the judgment. Those who lived during the Dark Ages, a time when Satan nearly extinguished the light of truth, could understandably argue that they were deprived of the light that has shone upon us in the twentieth century. But God has said that when He shows each person the reason for the guilty verdict pronounced against him, "every knee shall bow to me, and every tongue shall confess to God. So then every one of us shall give account of himself to God" (Romans 14:11, 12). All will then see and confess that God has been fair in His dealings with humanity. As it is written, "The grace of God that bringeth salvation *hath appeared to all men*" (Titus 2:11, emphasis supplied).

We need this bigger picture in order to get a right perspective on God's character. God's larger perspective reveals that although we may indeed affect others for or against God, our influence will not be the determining factor in anyone's decision. Though our witnessing may indeed influence others in their decision, people will ultimately believe and choose what they want.

Abounding grace

We need to realize that God deals with every human being with complete equity. The Scriptures, rightly understood, help us to see that He is indeed "no respecter of persons" (Acts 10:34) and that He is dealing fairly with everyone.

It's true that some people are born under more favorable spiritual circumstances and environments than are others. It may appear that such are at an advantage, but this is not necessarily the case. In order to give everyone equal opportunity, God has built in the compensating factors of light, faith, and free will. These guarantees counterbalance the sinful deficiencies we have inherited from Adam. The biggest equalizing factor is that God deals with us on a sliding scale. This is evident from the scripture that declares "where sin abounded, grace did much more abound" (Romans 5:20). To the person who is living under sinful circumstances that have prevented him from receiving large amounts of spiritual light, God lengthens His arm of grace. For such a person, He is willing to overlook more of the natural defects and ignorance and cover them with His atoning blood (see Psalm 87:4, 6). He does not expect such spiritually under-privileged persons to perform that which is expected from those with greater light. But once the light of conviction is brought home to the soul on a given point of truth, the individual then becomes inexcusable for his ignorance. At that point, in the eyes of divine justice, one becomes totally responsible for his decision regarding that light (See Acts 17:30).

For example, my cousin might be saved although he violates the Sabbath commandment, eats pork, and enjoys social drinking because he has not had the light of conviction regarding these matters. But does that mean that I, a Seventh-day Adventist, can be saved if I join him in these practices? This is often where we run into trouble as God's chosen people. Although we have been privileged with great light, we often want to live like the world and be judged according to the same standard by which the world will be measured. But Jesus taught that "unto whomsoever much is given, of him shall be much required: and to whom men have committed much, of him they will ask the more" (Luke 12:48). "Jesus, our Advocate, is acquainted with all the circumstances with which we are surrounded and deals with us according to the light we have had and the circumstances in which we are placed" (*Testimonies for the Church*, 2:74). To be willingly ignorant of what we know, deep down, is the truth will always lead us away from our commitment to God (see 2 Peter 3:5).

Sensible soul-saving

Never should we conclude that the salvation of others is totally dependent upon our efforts, as if God would let a person perish if we weren't around. This false concept can easily lead the self-sufficient to a pharisaical attitude of self-importance. On the other hand, this idea also often causes a decrease of witnessing activity by placing an undue burden upon our shoulders that results in a sense of futility. Many sincere souls burn out doing the Lord's work because they don't have a clear understanding of this matter.

It is often said in Adventist circles that persons will approach us in heaven because they will realize that if it weren't for what we did for them down here they would have been lost. Have you ever wondered why we will cast at the feet of Jesus our jewel-laden crowns (which represent the souls to whom we had a part in bringing the gospel message)? Because that's where they belong! People will not be there because of us but because of Him. There might even be a few that are there in spite of us!

God doesn't need any Uzzahs who feel that the security and success of His work of saving souls revolves around them alone. To say that someone will perish eternally if we are not involved makes us, in essence, the saving element. Such an attitude actually disqualifies us to be a stable element in the work the Lord is trying to accomplish on the earth. What God is really looking for is people who will humbly take hold of His work as though the eternal destinies of others depended upon their labors but who realize that opportunities to witness are a divine privilege. "One soweth, and another reapeth" (John 4:37). God could communicate His truth to those in darkness by writing it on a flower or leaf, or even in the sky. He could speak it to them audibly or send any one of His trillions of angels to convey it. Oh humbling and glorious thought, that when God has a soul ready for more light, He would think to send me! He works with people from their birth, preparing them to receive saving light. Then when the time comes, He lets you or me throw the switch! Yet often we walk away from such encounters polishing our halos of importance. Christian witnessing is a God-given privilege! When we taste just how sweet such an experience is, we will then be in constant prayer for more opportunities.

However, we must be careful in regard to these ideas. The

natural response of our hearts will be to say, "Well, if God is going to save souls with or without me, then I may as well go off and do my own thing." But the Lord has given us clear marching orders in this regard. Jesus said, "Go ye therefore, and teach all nations, baptizing them in the name of the Father, and of the Son, and of the Holy Ghost: teaching them to observe all things whatsoever I have commanded you" (Matthew 28:19, 20). If we give up our zeal for soul winning just because we discover that we are not the main cog in salvation's wheel, then I would sincerely question whether we had the right motives to begin with. Why would we ever struggle with letting God be the One who gets the glory in it all?

We must be as Paul, who because of God's goodness toward him, felt indebted to others and put forth all that was in him to preach the gospel to them (see Romans 1:14, 15). If we shirk this Christian duty of sharing saving light with those in darkness, then we will be held accountable to God in the judgment just as though the souls we neglected had been left to perish eternally. Most assuredly, "to save souls should be the lifework of everyone who professes Christ" (*Testimonies for the Church*, 4:53).

By involving ourselves in soul saving we certainly shall not be the loser. For us, Christian witnessing is a win/win arrangement. In laboring for others, we not only play a real part in their salvation process but are most assuredly working out our own salvation as well. "Those who are watching for souls, who devote themselves most fully to the salvation of the erring, are most surely working out their own salvation" (*Testimonies for the Church*, 5:606). In fact, the only way to grow in grace is to get involved in helping others through Christian service (see *Steps to Christ*, 80).

A true understanding of our role in the process of saving others, though it may discourage the Pharisee within us, will actually lead us to become more dependent upon God in our witnessing efforts. It will make the work of Christian witnessing even more enjoyable as we learn to place the real burden of saving souls upon the only One who can do it—the Lord Jesus. It will cause us to lift Him up to others all the more as their only hope of salvation and the grandest object of their adoration and respect. Such a realization will also cause us to value more highly the religious freedom of every person to choose to follow Jesus or to choose not to follow Him. It will help prevent us from using force, fear, or flattery in order to make our witnessing endeavors successful.

Marvelous grace of our loving Lord,
Grace that exceeds our sin and our guilt!
Yonder on Calvary's mount outpoured—
There where the blood of the Lamb was spilt.

Sin and despair, like the seawaves cold,
Threaten the soul with infinite loss;
Grace that is greater— yes, grace untold—
Points to the Refuge, the mighty Cross.

Dark is the stain that we cannot hide,
What can avail to wash it away?
Look, there is flowing a crimson tide;
Whiter than snow you may be today.

Marvelous, infinite, matchless grace,
Freely bestowed on all who believe!
You that are longing to see His face,
Will you this moment His grace receive?

Grace, grace, God's grace,
Grace that will pardon and cleanse within;
Grace, grace, God's grace,
Grace that is greater than all our sin!
—Julia H. Johnston

CHAPTER 6

The Responsibility of Freedom

In 1989 the world was stunned by satellite images of young people dancing atop the Berlin wall. Eastern Europe had begun celebrating its freedom from the oppressive rule of communism. I happened to view the historic event from a hotel room in Portland, Oregon. Later that evening I phoned my good friend, David Merrill, to get his assessment of the day's news. I've never forgotten his keen observation. He said, "I'm thankful that the people now have the opportunity to taste freedom for themselves. But in the long term, I think they will find that *with much freedom comes much responsibility*."

That insightful statement has proven true. In the years following the liberation of these nations, the world has watched them teeter economically like toddlers trying to walk for the first time. As inflation soared, they found that in a free market society, providing for even the necessities of life was not as easy as the Western world made it appear. Before long many of their citizens began to suggest a return to communism. "At least," they argued, "under the old regime one could depend upon the government to shoulder responsibility for basic provisions." Certainly, it's true that with much freedom comes much responsibility.

People often look in a similar way at the freedom Christians enjoy. When Adam and Eve fell, the human race was plunged under the tyranical rule of the kingdom of sin. Then Jesus came to liberate us through the atonement made at Calvary. Many churches have manufactured a gospel of easy religion and marketed it to the world. Such concepts as "just believe" and "once saved, always saved" have become the standard of belief in many quarters. Such sayings are founded upon a certain amount of truth, but the general understanding they convey is erroneous. As a result, few Christians today realize that responsibility comes along with their freedom in Christ.

Many think that once a person becomes a Christian, the remainder of life will be a bed of roses. They fail to realize that when they embrace the freedom of the Christian life, they still have a carnal nature to deal with, although they have been justified by Christ's saving blood. The well-known preacher Dwight L. Moody said,

> When I was converted I made this mistake. I thought the battle was already mine, the victory already won, the crown already in my grasp. I thought the old things had passed away, that all things had become new, and that my old, corrupt nature, the old life was gone. But I found out, after serving Christ for a few months, that conversion was only like enlisting in the army— that there was a battle on hand (*Life Sentence*, 21).

I myself passed through a similar experience shortly after becoming a Christian. I had the preconceived idea that life would get better when I accepted the truth that was to set me free. Instead, it seemed as though my sinful condition worsened. Negative character traits appeared to intensify and faults were revealed that I didn't even suspect existed. It seemed the harder I tried to be good, the more rotten I became. This would often plunge me into periods of deep depression. The agony was some-times so intense that I felt I could bear it no longer.

Feeling like a total failure as a Christian, I decided one night to return to the rottenness of my former life. I remember telling my wife that I just wasn't cut out to be a Christian and that she needed to go ahead and make her plans accordingly. Maybe others were good enough to make it, I told her, but me . . . I was resigned to a life of hell! Then I left the house in a determined search to find my former follies and return to the "freedom and security" of the old way of living.

Yet it didn't take long to discover that now I couldn't even enjoy my old sins the way I used to. I was like a prisoner of sheer despair. Caged within the confines of a knowledge of the truth, I had nothing to look forward to except "a certain fearful looking for of judgment and fiery indignation" (Hebrews 10:27). In a state of frenzied hostility to God, I cried out, "Leave me alone! Leave me alone! You wouldn't help me when I wanted to be a Christian, and now You won't even let me enjoy my sins!" Then I began to weep in bitter agony.

I don't remember how long this state of mental horror lasted. All I know is that I cried until I didn't feel like crying anymore. When my anguish calmed, I was sitting in my car on a grocery store parking lot. The rain was pouring down in torrents. As I looked up, I saw a pay phone underneath the eaves of the store. I felt desperate to talk to someone who might be able to make some sense out of my confusion.

At that moment I thought of an old Adventist pastor I had heard preach the year before in Tennessee. I got out of the car, ran to the pay phone, got his number from directory assistance, and called him. When he answered the phone, I found that all I could do was to start crying again. Although he didn't know me, he knew I was a soul in desperation. He pleaded with me to go ahead and cry but to "not hang up." When I regained my composure, he said, "Now, son, tell me what's wrong."

I then blurted out, "Well, pastor, I thought that when I became a Christian I was supposed to get better. But ever since I gave my life to Christ, I've been getting worse."

Once again entreating me not to hang up, he quickly went to his library to get a book from which he said he would like to read something to me. Upon returning, he asked me if I was familiar with the book *Steps to Christ*. I told him I was. He began reading from pages 64 and 65: "The closer you come to Jesus, the more faulty you will appear in your own eyes; for your vision will be clearer, and your imperfections will be seen in broad and distinct contrast to His perfect nature. This is evidence that Satan's delusions have lost their power; that the vivifying influence of the Spirit of God is arousing you" (64, 65).

Then the pastor told me something I shall never forget as long as I live. He said, "Now listen to me, son. It isn't that you're getting worse; you've been that bad all along! What is happening is that you've made a willing choice to follow Jesus. Now the Holy Spirit is showing you your constant need for God's grace. He is doing this by allowing you to see the stark contrast between Jesus' beautiful, holy character and the hideousness of your sinful nature. This is the way He is developing within you both a desire to be pure and a perfect hatred for sin."

I thought about this for a minute. Then I asked, "Are you sure?"

With a slight chuckle he said, "Listen, my young friend, you may think you are bad, but you're a whole lot worse than you think you are! But that's OK; Jesus knows all about it. You just take courage, because He is obviously working in your life."

Strangely, this paradoxical information was the most wonderful news I'd ever heard. To think that the great God of heaven was really on my side and not against me. I once again broke down and wept. But this time the tears were tears of joyful repentance that I had doubted His love and concern for me that evening.

Thus I learned my first big lesson concerning God's plan to save. Since that time I have come to understand even more that God's plan is a fair one. It is the only way by which anyone can be saved. We cannot devise a better way. All our attempts to do so will surely fail. Trying to invent another gospel will inevitably lead us into one of two errors. Either we will make the plan too lenient toward our sinful state, thus giving us a false security, or as I experienced that evening in the rain, we will set up an idealistic state of holiness that we must achieve in this life, eventually causing us to become utterly discouraged in trying to live up to it. We must forever be reconciled to the fact that God has already, in His own mind, solved the sin problem. He has devised the best and only possible way for us to escape it. Our part is to study to show ourselves approved. Then as workmen who rightly divide the word of truth, we are to cooperate with our findings. As we intelligently bring our wills under the influence of the plan, our salvation will be worked out, although with fear and trembling.

No doubt the biggest mistake we make is in trying to understand the plan of salvation from a human perspective. Our biggest struggle is in properly understanding just how the Lord is dealing with us. Because we are selfish by nature, we are prone to weave selfish principles into our understanding of the gospel. The result is that we mar what God is attempting to accomplish in our behalf. "This robe [the robe of Christ's righteousness that is to cover the nakedness of our sinful state], woven in the loom of heaven [designed by God in heaven], has in it not one thread of human devising" (*Christ's Object Lessons*, 311). It is highly essential that we view the plan of salvation from a universal perspective as heaven sees it. Thus our minds will be lifted above our selfish state, enabling us to see more clearly God's practical outline of salvation. This higher plane can be found only through a total reliance on the inspired writings.

Satan, of course, is determined we shall never do this. He

trembles to think that we might ever clearly see the plan in its divine beauty. He knows that if we discover the logical framework of God's design to save us, his power over us will be broken. Once we escape Satan's snares, our passion in life will be to help others get untangled. The devil cannot control our will. Therefore, he constantly seeks to divert our minds from a saving knowledge of the gospel. This is the real secret behind the introduction into our homes and churches of worldly activities and programs devoid of the Spirit. All Satan has to do is to keep the minds of God's people occupied until their sealing opportunity is past, and his purpose will be accomplished (see *Testimonies to Ministers*, 472-475).

As heaven sees it

Here is where a deeper understanding of the great controversy comes into play. Often we limit our prophetic interpretation to identifying the beast and warning people not to receive its mark. But an intellectual understanding of what the mark of the beast is will not prevent anyone from receiving it. The only way a person can be sure he will not receive the beast's mark is to have his name enrolled in the Lamb's book of life (see Revelation 13:8). And the only way that can happen is to have Jesus' saving blood atonement applied to his account in heaven's record book. That blood is our *only* hope of salvation. All we as sinful beings can do for our salvation is to accept by faith that blood on our behalf.

Yet we must never entertain the unbiblical thought that just because we are saved solely through faith that we are no longer under obligation to obey God's holy law. We must never lessen our views of the law's importance, even though we understand that it cannot save us. The genuine result of the gospel of grace is to transform our antagonistic attitudes about God's system of law and order. Grace seeks to make us responsible citizens of God's kingdom.

"Order is heaven's first law" (*Counsels on Health*, 101). It is law that preserves heaven's order, just as it is in our society. And God's law is a constitutional law much like the United States Constitution. The principles of that document, principles that the enemies of church-state separation constantly seek to alter, have been the secret of this nation's governing power and prosperity. Two of the grandest of those principles are the "right of self-government" and "freedom of religious faith" (*The Great Controversy*, 441).

These same rights—self-government and religious faith—are also guaranteed us by the constitution of heaven. This is why the sovereign God of the universe Himself has vowed not to tamper with the human will. In no way will He be mind for His intelligent creatures. Rest assured there are no "beast" policies in heaven.

However, law must be enforced in heaven just as it is on earth, else the breakdown of social order would result. Thus, the entrance of sin has placed the Monarch of the universe in a terrible predicament. God is both our Father and our Governor. As our Father, He loves us unconditionally and has a willingness to forgive us unconditionally. This is seen in the heart cry of the "everlasting Father" (Isaiah 9:6) when He cried out on the cross in behalf of those who were totally unrepentant, "Father, forgive them; for they know not what they do" (Luke 23:34). As we saw earlier, His love for us is so strong that it led Him to risk His own eternal existence in an effort to save us.

But there is one thing God cannot do, even in an effort to alleviate His own need to save us. He will in no way alter or bend the claims of the law in order to accommodate our sinful condition. As a Judge, He cannot forgive unconditionally, in the legal sense of the term, those who still intend to transgress His law. To do so would bring destruction upon the entire universe, because "upon conformity to these principles [of God's law] the well-being of the universe depends" (*Thoughts From the Mount of Blessing*, 48).

We have all by choice been involved in the experience of sin. That is why, whether we realize it or not, we each stand guilty of committing treason against the government of the universe. We've all heard about spies who sell secrets to foreign governments. Spies are despised and brought to justice for a good reason. They threaten the life of our state. If convicted, they are handed the severest penalty because their crime threatens all citizens and jeopardizes the entire existence of our country. Treason is the one crime mentioned in the United States Constitution.

But at this point, some might object, saying, "Wait a minute! I'm not a Benedict Arnold. I haven't done such awful things!" Most of us are unaware of the treason we commit against the heavenly universe in our sinful state. The consequences of a single sin have the capacity to destroy the entire universe. Remember that the present sin problem with all its misery and suffering evolved from a single thought in a single creature. Just as one cell infected with the AIDS virus can eventually destroy the whole body, so one rebellious heart that is determined to be selfish and live without respect for the rights of others has the capacity to undermine and dissolve the entire intelligent society of the universe. We each truly are the chief of sinners (see 1 Timothy 1:15).

Yet "for one sinner Jesus would have yielded up his life" (*General Conference Bulletin*, December 1, 1895). This high value that God places on a single soul is what makes the immensity of the plan of salvation so great. It's also the importance and potential influence of a single soul, for either good or evil, that provokes the fiercest battles in the great controversy. "If Satan sees that he is in danger of losing one soul, he will exert himself to the utmost to keep that one. . . . But if the one in danger perseveres, and in his helplessness casts himself upon the merits of the blood of Christ, our Saviour listens to the earnest prayer of faith, and sends a reinforcement of those angels that excel in strength to deliver him" (*Testimonies for the Church*, 1:345, 346).

Most often we think of the great controversy as being fought on a broader scale. Yet its real victories and defeats are actually determined by single cases. For example, a large portion of the angel force originally defected with the disgruntled Lucifer (see *The Story of Redemption*, 18). Can you imagine what power such infidelity had? But through His gracious appeals, God succeeded in fully winning back some, one by one. Consequently, when the need to protect the order of heaven finally required the removal of the defectors from the society they were poisoning, there were only one-third of God's treasured angels lost (see *Testimonies for the Church*, 5:291).

By this time, the lost angels were fully aware of what they had done and had no desire to do differently. I suppose that God could have used a little of His divine power to force those angels to come back to Him, but that's the whole point. Even though He had an intense desire to once again enjoy the companionship that only those individual angels could give Him, He cherished above all else their freedom to choose. Yet we can be sure that He used every honest persuasion possible to win them back.

So, on Earth Eve chose Satan's concept of unconditional freedom, which refuses to be subject to the rights of others, and took something that wasn't hers. This began a rebellion that spread to her husband, the influence of which caused the demise of the entire human race. Why didn't God immediately destroy Adam and Eve, or Cain? He didn't do so for two reasons.

First, in spite of His desire to save all future generations from ensuing heartache, He had to show how pervasive one wrong choice could be. That one wrong choice ultimately led to the destruction of the entire world by a Flood.

Second, divine love is always seeking to avoid amputation. Even before mankind sinned, a plan was in place to postpone the execution of the deserved justice. This probationary time granted divine agencies the opportunity of influencing fallen creatures to re-think their position and choose life instead of death.

So God gives us a second chance in Jesus, even though it's been such an incredible, fiendish work that we've done. He is dealing with each of us, as it relates to our personal salvation, as if we were the only person on earth. We need to realize that He is dealing with us on that one-to-one basis in order to truly appreciate Him as a personal Savior. And He wants to give us a personal pardon, signed by the Majesty of heaven and delivered by heaven's great diplomat, Jesus Christ. But the responsibility to choose freedom is up to each person individually. We cannot choose for others, only for ourselves. Yet the nature of our decision will automatically influence all who come within our sphere of existence. Thereby we either aid or hinder what God is attempting to accomplish in the lives of others.

Though we have a sinful nature, God still guarantees us freedom of choice through the Cross. He provides the infrastructure to keep us alive so we can hash out these issues as they relate to us personally. We're all set up with the neccessities of life—air, water, food, an inner sense of right and wrong, and liberty to choose. Everything we need in order to make our decision is granted us unconditionally through the Cross and the mighty Mediator. But He won't choose for us. Instead, He calls. The Holy Spirit is calling. He gives us the invitation "Come unto me." Revelation urges us to " 'Come' . . . take the water of life freely" (Revelation 22:17). It's open house in the sanctuary of God. Shall we not go in and see what He is offering?

Spirit of faith, come down, Reveal the things of God;
And make to us the God-head known, And witness with the blood.
'Tis Thine the blood to apply, And give us eyes to see,
Who did for ev'ry sinner die, Hath surely died for me.

The Responsibility of Freedom

No man can truly say, That Jesus is the Lord,
Unless Thou take the veil away, And breathe the Living Word.
Then, only then, we feel, Our interest in His blood,
And cry, with joy unspeakable, "Thou art my Lord, my God!"

O that the world might know, The all atoning Lamb!
Spirit of faith, descend and show, The virtue of His Name.
The grace which all may find, The saving pow'r, impart;
And testify to all mankind, And speak in ev'ry heart.

Charles Wesley

CHAPTER

7

Peaceful Negotiations

On November 4, 1979, the U.S. Embassy in Tehran was seized by Iranian militant students, and sixty-six U.S. employees were taken hostage. The students demanded that the former shah, who had taken refuge in the United States, be returned to Iran for trial. The Iranian government of Ayatollah Khomeini, who had taken power in February 1979 after the overthrow of the shah, warmly supported the students.

Immediately, the United States government, under the administration of President Jimmy Carter, began to seek a peaceful resolution to the crisis. Although the shah left the United States in early December, the militants refused to release their hostages. With diplomatic negotiations failing, Carter ordered a secret military rescue on April 24, 1980. The attempt failed and served only to heighten the tension between the two countries. Even the death of the shah in July 1980 had no effect on the hostages' status. It began to look more and more as though the crisis would break into open war as Carter re-instituted the military draft.

One year passed since the initial takeover of the embassy. Then in November 1980, the Iranian parliament set forth a list of conditions for the release of the hostages. Algeria was named mediator, and an agreement was finally signed in January 1981. On January 20, the day of Ronald Reagan's inauguration as president, the hostages were released. Thus a potentially bloody confrontation was resolved through peaceful negotiations.

From the standpoint of the universe, something similar has happened in our world. Planet Earth has been taken hostage by sin. From the beginning, God has possessed the power to invade and put down rebellion, just as the United States had the power to subdue the Iranian government in that crisis. Instead, God has chosen a different strategy in dealing with the secession of our world. For 6,000 years, now, God has been trying to convince as many of us sinful rebels as He possibly can to accept His terms of peace. He can do this because He paid the price of our sins at Calvary. In light of this sacrifice, time after time He has sent His ambassadors to communicate the terms of reconciliation—Enoch, Noah, Moses, Elijah, Isaiah, Jeremiah, Ezekiel, Daniel, Hosea, Zechariah, John the Baptist, Peter, John, Paul, and in our day, Ellen White. Yet because of human obstinancy, heaven has witnessed the cruel mocking and destruction of many of these chosen messengers.

At one point in the crisis, God Himself came and tried to communicate the terms of reconciliation. The Scriptures tell us, "Jesus began to preach, and to say, Repent: for the kingdom of heaven is at hand" (Matthew 4:17). Incredible thought! That the President of the universe, the heavenly Prince of Peace, should schedule a visit to our little planet! And He set up peace talks right there at Camp David, in Jerusalem! Surely in the end no one will ever be able to say that heaven hasn't exhausted every logical means of diplomacy in an attempt to make peace with the fallen race.

Yet it is absolutely amazing that, even today, few really understand the issues of the settlement heaven is proposing. We need to take time out of our busy lives and make it a top priority to learn what God is trying to say to us. Then our eyes will be opened to see what heaven is really offering. Only then will we make our peace with God and receive His power. Then, as His ambassadors, we will turn and present heaven's offer of peace to the whole world with a loud cry.

The document

The book of Hebrews is an amazing document. Adventist believers found direction, hope, and a sure word when that book was opened to them in a special way more than a hundred years ago. It mapped out clearer than ever the mission of the mighty diplomat to this world, Jesus Christ. It revealed His work, and most importantly, it opened to view the diplomatic papers of accord He brought down here to present to this alien province.

Hebrews presents Jesus both as a sacrificial Lamb and as the only Mediator to present Himself before the throne of the universe in our behalf. But Jesus's mediation has nothing to do with trying to bring about a change in God's heart. He is not trying to alter the Father's attitude toward us. Christ doesn't stand before Him in an attempt to satisfy His whims or arbitrary anger.

As mentioned earlier, God is our Father. As our Father, He loves each of us unconditionally, forever, regardless of our wrong decisions. As soon as the human race had a head-on collision with sin, the Father was in Christ reconciling the world to Himself. "The atonement of Christ [the means of His mediation] was not made in order to induce God to love those whom He otherwise hated; it was not made to produce a love that was not in existence; but it was made as a manifestion of the love that was already in God's heart" (*Signs of the Times*, 30 May 1895).

What is the major purpose for Christ's mediation then? *It is to bring about a change in our relation to the law and its penal function of justice.* This is accomplished as the Holy Spirit begins to apply to our minds the truths of His saving grace and affect a change in our rebellious attitudes toward the pronouncement of death that the law had to proclaim.

We must realize that although God loves us unconditionally, He has to maintain universal justice in order to preserve the stability of His government and of social relations throughout the universe and for all eternity. Christ's mighty mediation is designed to demonstrate His ability to bring us into harmony with the law without the use of force. This is necessary in order that He might credibly clear our case before the eyes of the citizens of the universe.

We who possess sinful natures are holding the universe hostage in our unwillingness to negotiate peace. We are determined that our demands be met. When it comes to giving up our sinful thoughts, secret ambitions, and selfish behavior, we often refuse even to come to the bargaining table. Little do we realize that in trying to hang on to what we consider valuable in this world, we are actually acting against the welfare of the universe and forfeiting our only opportunity to live eternally.

We find much to cling to in our sinful condition. Sometimes it's our money and material possessions. Sometimes it's our pride of knowledge. Others find self-redemption in their physical appearance or talents. Often it is an unwillingness to break away from cherished human relationships that stand between us and God. Others stubbornly hang on to pleasurable lifestyle practices that war against the mind and soul. But perhaps what sickens God's heart the most is our spiritual pride—pride in the success of our gospel work, along with the corresponding attitude that the church can't get along without us. A number of things, large or small, could be the thing we selfishly hold in preference to a total commitment of bringing our lives into conformity to the Lord's revealed will. This is why the Lord stated, "He that findeth his life shall lose it: and he that loseth his life for my sake shall find it" (Matthew 10:39).

Whatever our personal hangup may be, we've all committed terrorism against the unfallen society of the universe. And so Jesus came to our world with a document containing the conditions of peace. It is what we call a covenant, and it is folded in His arms next to His heart because that's where He wants us to be. Theologians tell us that the title on the opening page of this document reads, "Justification by Faith." As the apostle Paul so aptly put it, "Being justified by faith, we have peace with God" (Romans 5:1). That is a summary of what is in the document. This beautiful accord is stated in its most attractive light in these words:

> Being justified freely by His grace through the redemption that is in Christ Jesus: whom God hath set forth to be a propitiation through faith in his blood, to declare his righteousness for the remission of sins that are past, through the forbearance of God; to declare, I say, at this time his righteousness: that he might be just, and the justifier of him which believeth in Jesus (Romans 3:24-26).

Today, it is popular in some Christian circles to believe and teach that all humanity was legally justified at the Cross two thousand years ago. In other words, everyone's sins were unconditionally pardoned in the record books of heaven as a result of Christ's sacrifice. No doubt, this idea results from trying to harmonize God's fairness with the error that we were all eternally condemned as a result of the first Adam's choice. Obviously, if I am condemned on the basis of Adam's sin without any choice on my part, then I may be justified on the basis of Jesus' atonement without any choice on my part either.

But if we are going to use the term *justification,* we need to have a standard for what this legal expression means. Obviously, *justice* is the root of the word. Justice means fair and impartial treatment before law. Therefore, justification is justifying someone's right to exist although he has committed heinous crimes and deserves to die. Although in His mercy God treats sinners as innocent people, He cannot, justly, declare them innocent before the universe when they have no desire to be so. Due process of law does not permit unconditional justification or acquittal. To justifiy or acquit unconditionally would indicate that in some way the initial charges were unfair and that the one so charged deserves to be let off.

If sinners were acquitted of their alleged crimes before due process was carried out, that would be an obstruction of justice. The desire of the rebellious heart to bring the object of its rebellion (in this case God's law) to its terms would be granted, and sin would be excusable. If God, in carrying out His role as Judge, legally forgives one rebellious human or angel without their repentance, then He has given rebellious Lucifer what He demanded in the first place. The sinner is thus justified in his sins. To announce before the universe that such a one has legally been cleared, acquitted, and affirmed in his sins, with his devious plots unchecked, would be unjust. It would be comparable to the United Nations granting amnesty to all known terrorists in the world. What a message of fear this would send to the universe—that God's divine government won't hold criminals personally accountable for their criminal attitudes and behavior.

This is why Ellen White has told us

> Satan deceives many with the plausible theory that God's love for His people is so great that He will excuse sin in them. . . . The *unconditional pardon of sin never has been, and never will be.* Such pardon would show the abandonment of the principles of righteousness, which are the very foundation of the government of God. It would fill the unfallen universe with consternation. . . . That so-called benevolence which would set aside justice is not benevolence but weakness (*Patriarchs and Prophets*, 522, emphasis supplied).

We must never disrupt the delicate equation in which God deals with this matter of justice and mercy. Although He does indeed keep mercy for thousands and forgives iniquity and transgression and sin, He "will by no means clear the guilty" (Exodus 34:7). The hard, fast truth is that if we remain unrepentant and determined in our sinful course, God "will not forgive [our] transgressions nor [our] sins" (Joshua 24:19). A gospel of unconditional salvation will always lead us into the religion of Babylon, just as surely as will the belief that our works play a role in meriting our salvation.

Salvation is provisionary (see *Selected Messages*, 1:375). The blood of Jesus is always available, but the choice is ours. God will not force a peace agreement between us and heaven. If peace is ever made, it will come as a result of our intelligent cooperation and not by an arbitrary proclamation of amnesty by God. While Calvary brings us many benefits, unconditional, legal forgiveness, though seemingly a friendly concept, is really a stranger to God's government of personal responsibility.

The Lord has calculated that a correct knowledge of His character of selfless love is the strongest incentive to lead the alienated human heart to sign the peace document of its own free will. But there are terms to His proposed agreement. "God has made every provision to bring salvation within our reach, but He will not thrust it upon us against our will. He has laid down conditions in His word, and we should diligently, interestedly, with heart and mind, set about the task of learning these conditions, lest we make some mistake and fail to secure our title to the mansions above" (*Testimonies for the Church*, 5:542).

The terms

The nature and presentation of God's terms differ from human offers based on terms. God is not standing aloof from us and saying, "All right, here is what you have to do, and when you meet the terms, then I will give you salvation." The Lord knows we are sinful by nature and cannot possibly meet the terms of salvation's agreement. All He wants is a willingness on our part to cooperate with Him. As the scripture says, "If there be first a willing mind . . ." (2 Corinthians 8:12). We often make the conditions of salvation more difficult than God ever intended them to be. Inspiration describes them as "gracious and liberal terms" (*Signs of the Times*, 15 January 1885). Never should we think of the terms for making peace with God as a roadblock in coming to Him. While it is uncontrovertible that salvation is conditional, "the conditions of obtaining mercy of God are simple and just and and reasonable" (*Steps to Christ*, 37).

It is our biblical privilege to have assurance in Christ. In order to have peace and sanity in this world of uncertainty, every follower of Christ needs to know with assurance that his title to glory is secure. And as long as we realize our utter dependence on Christ, we are privileged to proclaim that assurance in full faith. God wants us to realize that in the arms of Jesus we are safe and secure. That is why He reassures us over and over again through such Bible promises as "All that the Father giveth me shall come to me; and him that cometh to me I will in no wise cast out" (John 6:37).

Building upon this promise, Ellen White wrote, "If you have nothing else to plead before God but this one promise from your Lord and Saviour [John 6:37 quoted], you have the assurance that you will never, never be turned away. . . . Present this assurance to Jesus, and you are as safe as though inside the city of God" (*Manuscript Releases*, 10:175). Amazing! Whatever crisis we find ourselves in, by turning to God in faith, we are as safe down here as Enoch, Moses, and Elijah are in heaven.

But there is something that is just as bad as no assurance, and that is false assurance.

Let it not be forgotten that those who bring their petitions to God, claiming his promises, while they do not comply with the conditions, insult Jehovah.... Many have no assurance of acceptance with him. They have forfeited, and are continuing to forfeit, the conditions upon which acceptance is based. . . . They approach God with his promises, and ask him to fulfil them, when by so doing he would dishonor his name (*Southern Watchman*, 4 June 1903).

Our faith is to be an intelligent faith. Only then will we know that our standing with God is sure and be able to successfully meet the enemy when he comes to challenge our faith.

All of heaven's terms for reconciliation are actually wrapped up in a single word—*faith*! But faith is a very encompassing word. Notice all that it involves:

Faith in Christ *is the only condition* upon which justification can be received; and the gift is bestowed *only* upon those who realize that they are sinners, and undeserving of mercy. The merits of the blood of Christ must be presented to the Father as the offering for the sins of men. *When* sinners seek God, and in repentance confess their sin, he pardons their transgressions, remits their punishment, and receives them into fellowship with himself, as if they had never transgressed. He imparts to them the righteousness of Christ (*The Youth's Instructor*, 1 March 1900, emphasis supplied).

Authentic faith, which is a gift from God, will always lead the believer to meet the conditions of salvation. A spurious faith, which is best identified as presumption, will seek to claim salvation while refusing to submit to all of faith's components. Yet there is no merit in either faith or repentance. They are simply the tools God provides us so that we can come into possession of the merits of Christ's saving blood.

Faith is more than an intellectual assent. It is an experience. God's credibility, as shown in His gift of Christ, creates unquestioning trust in Him. As we contemplate what He did for us, we will treasure Him so much that we will want to abandon everything in the world for Him. We enter into an intimate relationship with Him like we do when we get married. "For thy Maker is thine husband; the Lord of hosts . . . thy Redeemer" (Isaiah 54:5).

Remember those initial feelings of affection for the one you chose to be your life partner? Remember how he or she was all that you thought of or talked about. Remenber how you ached to be in his or her presence? Such intense emotional love would have led us to do anything in order to win the favor of our beloved!

This same series of emotions and feelings toward God is brought about by faith. Note this description of saving faith:

> The faith that is unto salvation is not a mere intellectual assent to the truth. . . . It is not enough to believe about Christ; we must believe in Him. The only faith that will benefit us is that which *embraces Him as a personal Saviour*, which appropriates His merits to ourselves. Many hold faith as an opinion. Saving faith is a transaction by which those who receive Christ join themselves in covenant relation [like a marriage] with God (*The Desire of Ages*, 347, emphasis supplied).

So we can see that the nature of saving faith is that of a marriage-type relationship. We can see that it is not a casual faith. This is a deep faith that involves a close, intimate relationship with God. And we can't form that kind of faith. We can't initiate or create it.

Then how does it happen?

The Bible says that such saving faith is a gift from our loving God. But the secret to receiving this gift of faith is in finally coming to the place in our busy lives that we rivet our undivided attention on the gift of His Son. Jesus said, "And I, if I be lifted up from the earth, will draw all men unto me" (John 12:32). Through the incarnated gift of Christ we see God giving Himself to His helpless creatures. As we begin to understand the significance of the infinite risk God took in order to give us such a gift, it will stimulate a response in our hearts like the one that the woman at the well experienced. It will open up our own wells of affection that have long been encrusted by selfishness and sin. It will bring us into a binding, marriage-type relationship with God through Christ.

Yet because of a long string of broken human relationships, many of us struggle to believe that such a relationship with God is even possible. However, the relationship God is speaking of here is not one that is based upon or built around human selfishness. It's like the tender story of Hosea's experience with his unfaithful Gomer. That heart-wrenching story is designed to teach us that God loves us with an unquenchable love. No matter how many times we have played the harlot and broken the relationship, He is waiting to redeem us. Ultimately, as Gomer realized her faithful husband's love was unshakable, we must confront the fact that the Godhead can't live without us. Much more than our earthly parents, God has proven that He will give up His own existence to draw us home.

Saving faith is created within us as we begin to appreciate and face this fact that God's personal love for us is stronger than death. When the barriers that our sin attitude have created are broken down by this gospel reality, we will turn to God in love. This is gospel repentance. In sorrow, we will confess our foolish pride and rebellious attitudes toward Him and others in detail (spontaneous confession). Then, and only then, will we proudly take a bold stand of unquestioning obedience to the commands of the One we now love and supremely admire with a deep heart reverence.

Some have made the conditions of salvation a cold list of requirements that we must achieve in order to be saved. Saving faith may take years to develop, its elements secretly brewing in the converted heart. Then, at some critical point, when the charms of God's love take us captive, the Holy Spirit brings together all these wonderful elements—repentence, confession, obedience, etc.—and suddenly, an intelligent, saving faith is born.

Thus at any moment the complete terms of God's covenant of grace may be fulfilled in our lives. And as long as the elements of this type of relationship exist and are growing in our hearts, we are eternally secure. "For by one offering he hath perfected for ever them that are sanctified" (Hebrews 10:14).

However, it should be noted that many in this wide world have not had the opportunity to hear and know the gospel reality of Jesus Christ. Romans, chapter 2, teaches us that from such God accepts the blind faith that is imperceptibly being created within them by the Holy Spirit's prompting. When anyone on this globe in faith opens his mind to the impressions of the Spirit, salvation occurs.

"Death entered the world because of transgression. But Christ gave His life that man should have another trial . . . to secure for man a second probation" (*Testimonies for Ministers*, 134). By means of Christ's mediation, we are granted a period of time in which we can study the offer of salvation and choose for ourselves whether or not we really want it. "The Lord gives men and women probationary time in which to acquaint themselves with His terms of salvation" (*Signs of the Times*, 24 June 1903). And we seriously will want to search out these things only when we understand that God is not arbitrary but is working on our behalf and is reasonable in His dealings with us. Then we will take hold of His strength and make peace with Him (see Isaiah 27:5; Romans 5:1).

SAVING BLOOD

There is a fountain filled with blood,
Drawn from Immanuel's veins;
And sinners plunged beneath that flood,
Lose all their guilty stains.

The dying thief rejoiced to see
That fountain in his day;
And there may I, though vile as he,
Wash all my sins away.

Thou dying Lamb! Thy precious blood
Shall never lose its power,
Till all the ransomed church of God
Are saved, to sin no more.

Lord, I believe Thou hast prepared,
Unworthy though I be,
For me a blood-bought, free reward,
A golden harp for me!

There in a nobler, sweeter song,
I'll sing Thy power to save,
When this poor lisping, stammering tongue
Is ransomed from the grave.
—William Cowper

CHAPTER
8

Investigating the Judgment—Part 1

Compared with the rest of the Christian world, Seventh-day Adventists hold certain unique doctrines. But the feature of our faith that really sets us apart centers around what has come to be known as the "investigative judgment." For more than one hundred fifty years, we have taught that when the 2,300 prophetic days ended Christ entered into the judgment phase of His heavenly ministration. Said the prophet Daniel, "I beheld till the thrones were cast down, and the Ancient of days did sit. . . . A fiery stream issued and came forth from before him: thousand thousands ministered unto him, and ten thousand times ten thousand stood before him: the judgment was set, and the books were opened" (Daniel 7:9, 10).

This concept of an end-time judgment is best understood as the fulfillment of the symbolism of the Day of Atonement in the Hebrew sanctuary service. In fact, it was primarily an understanding of how the earthly tabernacle services related to what is going on in heaven that catapulted the Advent movement into denominational existence. The role of Seventh-day Adventists, as a unique people with a special end-time message for the world, hinges upon the validity of our interpretation of the prophecies pertaining to the investigative judgment. One can understand why, then, the sanctuary doctrine has become one of the most debated topics both within and without our ranks.

Some have claimed that such a teaching is unbiblical. They have tried their best to prove that Daniel's prophecies were fulfilled sometime in the distant past and therefore have nothing to do with our day. But no one can get around the fact that the setting for Daniel's prophecies is the "time of the end," after the reign of the Roman papal government (see Daniel 12:4, 9, 13). As Daniel explained to the king of Babylon, "There is a God in heaven that revealeth secrets, and maketh known to the King Nebuchadnezzer what shall be *in the latter days*" (Daniel 2:28, emphasis supplied).

But more alarming than the external attacks on this doctrine is the indifference that so many Adventists themselves manifest toward the teaching of the investigative judgment. No doubt, this is due to the fact that many do not understand exactly what role this end-time judgment plays in the overall plan of salvation. Our lethargic attitude is why God allows controversy after controversy to come to us regarding this issue. By this means, an otherwise dead point of our faith is brought to the forefront and becomes the object of intense discussion and study. Historically, every time doctrinal controversy on this point has occurred, the church has emerged from the conflict more enlightened and convicted than ever that the doctrine of the investigative judgment is a sound, unshakable, biblical truth.

The timing of the atonement

The word *atonement* actually means "at-one-ment" with God, the means and the method whereby the sinner, separated from God by sin, is made one with God or reconciled to Him. This definition is not disputed among Bible scholars, but there are differences of opinion regarding the *timing* of the atonement. Due to our teaching of the investigative judgment and its corresponding work of the "final atonement," Seventh-day Adventists are often misunderstood. The evangelical Christian world teaches that the atonement was finished on the cross, whereas, historically, Adventists have held that the work of atonement extends (in a certain sense) to the close of Christ's mediatorial work in the heavenly sanctuary.

Ellen White seemed to consider both views as having some validity. In one place she speaks of the close of probation as the time "when the work of atonement in the heavenly sanctuary has been completed" (*The Great Controversy*, 658). Yet, she also wrote regarding Calvary, "When the Father beheld the sacrifice of His Son, He bowed before it in recognition of its perfection. 'It is enough,' He said. *'The Atonement is complete'* "(*Review and Herald*, 24 September 1901, emphasis supplied). Failure to balance such statements have led to fierce debates among Adventists.

Most of the misunderstanding in this regard has been a matter of semantics. It is not uncommon for an identical term associated with the plan of salvation to have multiple connotations and to be applicable to different time periods. Take for example the word *redemption*. Because of his faith in what Christ did at Calvary, it is quite appropriate for the Christian to say "I have been redeemed." It is equally proper for him to say "I am being redeemed," in reference to biblical sanctification, the process whereby the life is purified from enslaving habits through faithful obedience to God's Word (see Acts 2:47, RSV). And yet the same Christian can also view redemption as something yet future. Speaking of His second coming, Jesus told His followers to "look up . . . for your redemption draweth nigh" (Luke 21:28). This is obviously referring to "the redemption of our body" at Christ's second advent (Romans 8:23).

The same principle applies to the use of the word *atonement*. Just as there are different phases of Christ's redeeming work, so there are different phases relating to the work of atonement. Jesus' death as the sacrificial Lamb at Calvary was for the purpose of paying the debt that humanity's sins had incurred. "Justice demanded that a certain price be paid" (E. G. White, Letter 20, 1903). That debt-paying sacrifice is called "the atonement." In this context, there should be no question that the atonement made at Calvary was a completed atonement. Jesus paid the full price for sin when He died on the cross. The sacrificial atonement made there by Christ was so perfect and efficacious that "it will never need to be repeated" (E. G. White, *SDA Bible Commentary*, 5:1132). The Bible says, "For in that He [Jesus] died, he died unto sin *once*." "So Christ was *once* offered to bear the sins of many" (Romans 6:10; Hebrews 9:28, emphasis supplied).

Adventism's emphasis on a "final atonement" has a connection with Christ's closing work in the heavenly sanctuary. But in no way should this connection and its purpose be presented in such a way as to cause others to think that we mean Christ must make another payment for sin's penalty or that His sacrifice on the cross was somehow incomplete or still in progress.

The final atonement is simply a legal recognition in the books of heaven that what Christ did at the Cross is covering the individual sinner's account. It is the time when the benefits of the Cross are affirmed as final and irrevocable, for all eternity, for those who have already recieved the atonement. Note, it is not the time when our personal atonement, reconciliation, or salvation occurs. This happens when we accept Christ and are converted. The issue of this final atonement is between God and the onlooking universe, not between God and the converted soul. This act is spoken of in the Bible as the blotting out of sins (Acts 3:19), the removal of sins from the life record. The sole purpose of the work of the investigative judgment is "an examination of the books of record to determine who, through repentance of sin and faith in Christ, are entitled to the benefits of His atonement" [on Calvary] (*The Great Controversy*, 422). It is also a cutoff point beyond which the atonement made by Christ on Calvary will no longer be made available to the fallen race.

This two-phase work of atonement is in keeping with the services of the earthly sanctuary. There was a morning and evening sacrifice offered in behalf of all the people. This represented the sacrifice that Christ made for the sins of all humanity. In this way, atoning blood was made available for all, regardless of an individual's attitude toward the provision. But if someone wanted to personalize the atonement in his own behalf, he was required to bring a sacrifice to the sanctuary himself. Only by confessing and repenting of the sins he had personally committed could the sinner have his sins transferred into the sanctuary via the blood of his slain sacrifice. Though the atonement was provided for all, it would benefit only those who felt their need of pardon and repented of their sins.

So it is with us today. "Even now it is not too late for wrongs to be righted and for the blood of a crucified and risen Saviour to atone in your behalf if you repent and feel your need of pardon" (*Testimonies for the Church*, 3:476). Here we again see that God did not, in a legal sense, corporately forgive eveyone at Calvary. Rather, He made ample provision so that anyone who wanted to obtain forgiveness could have it.

Day by day, as sacrifices were offered, the blood, symbolically bearing with it the confessed sins, was taken into the first apartment of the sanctuary. Although the sins had been transferred to the sanctuary at the time they were confessed, "the sin was not canceled by the blood of the victim" (*The Great Controversy*, 420).

This daily service in the earthly sanctuary symbolized Christ's work in the first apartment of the sanctuary in heaven, beginning at His ascension until judgment began in 1844. Inspiration tells us that "the blood of Christ, pleaded in behalf of penitent believers, secured their pardon and acceptance with the Father, yet their sins still remained upon the books of record" (*The Great Controversy*, 421).

Once a year, on the Day of Atonement, the sinner's future was disclosed. Sin records were then forever removed from the sanctuary, and "final judgment" for that year was made in behalf of those who were honest in their contrition. But if any had persisted in their unrepentant alienation, cleaving to and justifying their sinful life, then they would not be covered by the blood of the sacrifice, and would be unfortunately, "cut off" from God's inheritance.

Many have been scared away from this gospel teaching by the fact that our sins remain in the heavenly records until the final atonement takes place. They perceive this to mean that we are not secure in our forgiveness until the judgment. But Paul wrote, "*Now* is the accepted time; behold, *now* is the day of salvation" (2 Corinthians 6:2, emphasis supplied). We have "*now* received the atonement" (Romans 5:11, emphasis supplied). To believe in the concept of a final atonement at the end of time does not mean that we are waiting until some future time to receive our salvation. The final atonement is simply a reaffirmation by Christ of the earlier justification of those who have put their complete trust in the merits of His atoning blood. In fact, every glorious event related to the plan of redemption—be it the Lord's resurrection, His ascension, the outpouring of the Holy Spirit at Pentecost, the investigative judgment, or the Second Coming and its related resurection of the saints—all are but the fruit of what took place at Calvary.

Here is where a lot of confusion, frustration, and desperation concerning salvation has come in among Adventists. Somehow we have concluded from Ellen White's writings that we really don't have salvation until some distant time in the future after we have first proved ourselves by our righteous performance. We haven't felt sure that we have the security of the final atonement at conversion. But if we give ourselves to Christ at our conversion and determine to walk with Him, we have the final atonement right then and there, in essence. All we are waiting on is for some technical office work to be done by our Advocate. So "reckon ye also yourselves to be dead indeed unto sin" (Romans 6:11) and your case closed.

We need not wait until some future time to feel we have been made complete in Christ; we can claim it right now. "They [God's people] are not to look forward thinking that at some future time a great work is to be done for them; *for the work is now complete*" (*The Published Ellen G. White Writings*, 25, emphasis supplied). Yes, we Adventists, too, may feel at liberty to claim all those Bible promises that speak of our sins being gone from us the moment we accept Christ (see Isaiah 44:22; 55:7; Jeremiah 31:34; 50:20). It is our privelege, as well, to feel, as did the prodigal son, "that the past is forgiven and forgotten, blotted out forever" (*Christ's Object Lessons*, 204).

Why, then, are we told that our sins stay on record and rest in the sanctuary until the time of the final atonement? (see *Patriarchs and Prophets*, 357).

It all goes back to the point thatGod is not manipulating the situation, arbitrarily electing people to salvation against their choice. These records are not there to stack the cards against us, but to prove that God is not trying to sweep anything under the rug where an indivuals salvation is concerned. They are there to vindicate His gracious dealings and to leave things open should we change our mind about our relationship to Him. As far as God is concerned, the salvation deal is done the moment we accept Jesus as our personal Saviour. But He doesn't corral us into making such a decision and then refuse to let us out. He never forbids us from ever turning back to our old sinful ways. Such would be to say that once we are saved, we will always be saved. Instead, God has set it up through the sanctuary so that our decision, as it relates to Christ and sin, is not made irrevocable until we close our probationary period in this life. Our sins remain in the sanctuary in case we, like Balaam, *decide we want them back*. God has a money-back guarantee in the salvation transaction that says, "If at any time in the course of your lifetime you are not satisfied with My robe of righteousness, you may have your filthy rags back."

God loves free, open, intimate relationships. That's why He created marriage and gave it to us as an example of the kind of relationship He wishes to have with us. God dosen't deliberately do things to strain the relationship and threaten the "marriage." He's the One who gave us 1 Corinthians 13, which states that a love relationship "does not keep account of evil" and that "love knows no limits to its endurance, no end to its trust, no fading of its hope. It can outlast anything" (Phillips). In any love relationship, the option is always there for disillusionment and divorce to take place. And that is the loudest statement of rejection anyone can proclaim. If we come to the place that we lose our taste for God and His ways, He has no choice but to let us go back to our burdens and records of sin. But you can be sure He mourns in inexpressible anguish.

If at any time we decide that living with Christ is not what we really want, we are saying our relationship with Him is over. Then, sadly, the memories that up to that point reside in our album of love with Christ in the heavenly sanctury, will be just a painful picture in Gods heart, and there will remain nothing but our record of sin. Isn't this what Ezekiel 33:18 is really saying? When the reighteous turneth from his reighteousness, and committeth iniquity. . . all his righteousness shall not be remembered.

This only proves once again how much respect God has for our personal right to choose. It will prove to the universe that we have made no rash decisions but have chosen freely to become settled in our choice to be sons or daughters of God for eternity. It demonstrates that God is not trying to trap us into a saving decision but is trying His best to work with our freedom to choose, right down to the very end. The blotting out of our sins at the final atonement is really God's payday when He gets to enthusiastically tell the universe, "You see! I told you they were mine!"

When the investigative judgment is presented in a negative light, the impression comes across that God has a checklist of everything we need to do, or not to do, and that unless we cooperate we are not going to pass the judgment. As a result, we feel that He is going around with a jealous eye to discern our errors and mistakes, trying to find something that can keep us out of His holy kingdom. But such is a gross misrepresentation of our heavenly Father. It is a strategy the devil employs to keep us out of heaven (see *Steps to Christ*, 11). The investigative judgment is not an effort on God's part to see how many of us He can eliminate by making the way to heaven unreasonably difficult. Rather, it is to show the inhabitants of the universe, in the presence of Satan's accusing eye, that the souls desiring an entrance into heaven really do love Him and His ways.

Isn't that a strange situation—someone publicly investigating to see whether He can really have that which He has already purchased? But in the light of impartial law and Satan's scrutinizing eye, God must submit to such a process. Oh, how fearful an ordeal it is for Jesus to have His investment on the shipping dock of the church, bought and paid for with His own saving blood, only to have it put back in the stock of Satan's synogogue because by that person's choice he has decided that is really where he wants to be!

What I am trying to say is that we need to balance correctly our view between Calvary and the final atonement. As Adventists, there is a danger of a misguided attention to the final atonement at the expense of Calvary. If we are not careful, we can end up making the final atonement the end rather than focusing on Christ and His cross as means *and* the end—the "author and finisher of our faith" (Hebrews 12:2) and the object of our salvation. Accepting Christ's accomplishments on the cross assures us that we successfully pass the scrutiny of the judgment. If our hope is focused on the blood, these things are guaranteed! "For by one offering he hath perfected for ever them that are sanctified" (Hebrews 10:14).

The delay of judgment

Sometimes critics question why the judgment should occur at the end of time. However, there is a reasonable explanation why God has placed the judgment near the end of the world. As far as justice was concerned, judgment should have taken place the very day Adam sinned. But Christ willingly became "the Lamb slain from the foundation of the world" (Revelation 13:8), and by so doing postponed the judgment.

Because of their [Adam's and Eve's] transgression they were sentenced to suffer death, the penalty of sin. But Christ, the propitiation for our sins, declared: "I will stand in Adam's place. I will take upon myself the penalty of his sin. He shall have another trial. I will secure for him a probation. He shall have the priveleges and the opportunities of a free man, and be allowed to exercise his God-given power of choice. *I will postpone the day of his arraignment for trial*. He shall be bound over to appear at the bar of God in the judgment" (*Atlantic Union Gleaner*, 19 August 1903, emphasis supplied).

Though justice demanded immediate trial and execution, mercy sought to delay the court date. This was in harmony with God's purpose to open for man a way of escape. (see *Steps to Christ*, 62). Both justice and mercy lingered at Calvary. When they beheld the infinite sacrifice made in behalf of erring mortals, they threw their arms around each other and embraced with an eternal kiss of agreement. Both were satisfied because God, by legally paying the penalty for sin, could thereby save fallen man on the simple condition of faith. We have already discussed how such faith is produced by God's love and naturally leads us to an obedient attitude.

Just as the Bible prophets foretold the when, where, and how of Calvary, they likewise delivered to us necessary information concerning the postponed judgment of sinners. To them the judgment was a future event. The wise man exhorted us to keep God's commandments, "for God *shall bring* every work into judgment, with every secret thing, whether it be good, or whether it be evil" (Ecclesiastes 12:14, emphasis supplied). King David told us that God "hath prepared his throne for judgment. And he *shall judge* the world in righteousness" (Psalm 9:7, 8, emphasis supplied). Jesus Himself warned us that we would have to "give account thereof *in the day of judgment*" (Matthew 12:36, emphasis supplied) for even the words that we speak. While these statements speak of a future judgment, it has become popular to believe that "the day" of judgment was the day Jesus died on the cross and that it was for those who are "in Christ." There are important distinctions here. We must be careful how we interpret these verses so as not to steal from the converted soul his assurance in Christ, yet at the same time so as to avoid persumption. We are not being gradually saved and then saved wholly at the judgement. We are either totally saved now in Christ, or we are totally lost. So why did the apostle Paul, speaking several years after the cross, still preach of a "judgment *to come*" (Acts 24:25, emphasis supplied).

The Bible tells us that "the Lord God will do nothing, but he revealeth his secret unto his servants the prophets" (Amos 3:7). The Lord did not withhold any necessary information concerning the birth, life, death, and resurrection of Jesus. Neither was He vague in reference to the future judgment. Even the time when it was to begin was revealed through the prophet Daniel. We could call Daniel the "when" prophet. He disclosed *when* the Messiah would appear for His annointing and crucifixion in the midst of the seventieth week; he also told us *when* the postponed judgment would begin—at the end of 2,300 prophetic days.

That's why the Millerites announced to the world that "the hour of His judgment *is come*" (Revelation 14:7, emphasis supplied).

The biblical discovery of the sanctuary and its corresponding work of a pre-advent, investigative judgment has enabled God's last-day people to get a focus on that "complete system of truth" which is "connected and harmonious" (*The Great Controversy*, 423). Yet, many in the Advent movement today still question the validity of this doctrine. Such are often arbitarily condemned by church members for not believing in the traditional view of the judgment, as though they were terrible and wicked people.

But if one would get to the real core of their disbelief, it would often be revealed that they have had this doctrine presented to them in a negative light. As a result, they have come to associate the investigative judgment with an unreasonable God who is trying to make it difficult for people to get to heaven. It hasn't yet been made plain to them that it is the "Father's good pleasure to give [us] the kingdom" (Luke 12:32). The judgment is the event in which God, through the merits of Christ's saving blood, literally hands to the human race the keys to His eternal kingdom. Oh, if we could only realize that the judgment, so often feared and despised, is really God's golden opportunity to "pronounce . . . judgment in favour of the saints" (Daniel 7:22, NIV). The judgment is to be part of the everlasting gospel message that is to be given to the world here in the end (see Revelation 14:6, 7). The word *gospel* means "good news," so the judgment is to be good news to all who hear it. If it is not good news, then that should be an indicator that we have not yet connected the fact that by means of Christ's atoning blood we are to be cleared of the charges made against us.

It is often argued that God doesn't need to investigate to find out whose are His, because He said "I am the good shepherd, and know my sheep" (John 10:14). There is no doubt that being omniscient, God already knows who is faithful and who is not. But the investigative judgment is not for God's enlightenment. Rather, it is so His creatures throughout the universe might understand exactly what is going on regarding the decisions being made by members of the fallen race. God's government is a government of the people. He does nothing in the dark. He makes no secret decisions when it comes to the eternal welfare of the sinner; He invites all to "come . . . reason together" (Isaiah 1:18). The books have been faithfully kept and are now open for the inspection of all the citizens of God's universe.

The investigative judgment isn't so much to show *what we have been doing* as it is to reveal *who we have been loving*. It is the cosmic event in which God honors before the unfallen worlds the choices of all those who profess to serve Him on earth. It is an open court process whereby God reveals where our loyalties lie and whether we have responded to Christ's drawing love. When rightly understood, the doctrine of the judgment connects and uplifts Calvary as the only hope for anyone to be saved. But it also reveals the fact that we have freely chosen Christ in a personal decision based on persuasion, not coercion. It is our personal decision regarding what took place there that will determine our destiny in the end.

Though often disguised with an air of theological intellectualness, the underlying reason that many rise up among us and attempt to refute the doctrine of the investigative judgment is that it is the very doctrine that reveals that God considers us accountable beings. Many would rather believe that God, at Calvary, automatically releases us from our accountability. But the judgment message teaches that we are responsible for our sins and judgement bound. This reality is intended to drive us to Christ so that we can personally transfer that responsibility to Him and be aquitted of our crimes before the heavenly tribunal.

Just as God called Adam from his hiding place in Eden to face what he had done, the investigative judgment leaves no room for anyone to continue hiding behind fig leaves of self-deception. Those who believe they can go to Calvary and be saved through an unconditional gospel deceive themselves. They may be foremost in their apparent zeal for the religion of Christ. Yet when their profession is tested by investigation, it will be displayed that they still have a bone to pick with God over who is really responsible for sin.

As we shall see in our next chapter, if we are under Christ's saving blood, we have absolutely nothing to fear regarding the investigative judgment. It is an unfriendly doctrine only to those who refuse the very blood that can save them.

O solemn thought! And can it be, The hour of judgment is now come,
Which soon must fix our destiny, And seal the sinner's fateful doom?
Yes, it is so; the judgment hour Is swiftly hastening to its close;
Then will the Judge, in mighty power, Descend upon His foes.

He who came down to earth to die, An offering for the sins of men,
And then ascended up on high, And will ere-long return again,
Is standing now before the ark, And mercy seat, and cherubim,
To plead His blood for saints, and make The last remembrance of their sin.

The solemn moment is at hand, When we who have His name confessed,
Each in his lot must singly stand, And pass the final, searching test.
Jesus! we hope in Thee alone; In mercy now upon us look,
Confess our names before the throne, And blot our sins from out the book.

O blessed Saviour! May we feel, The full importance of this hour,

Investigating the Judgment—Part 1

Inspire our hearts with holy zeal, And aid us by Thy Spirit's
power,
That we may, in Thy strength, be strong, And brave the
conflict valiantly;
Then, on Mount Zion, join the song, And swell the notes of
victory.

R. F. Cottrell

CHAPTER
9

Investigating the Judgment—Part 2

In order to have a right view of how the judgment works and to avoid getting a false picture of God's fairness, it's important that we review a few points. At His first visit, Christ came to reveal the true feelings of the Father's heart toward us. God sent His Son to die for the sins of all human beings. This fact alone reveals that if it were left up to God, He would save everybody. But to save everyone, just because He loves them, would be to reject the authority of His law which states, "the soul that sinneth, it shall die" (Ezekiel 18:20).

So, just as God's love and His salvation are not synonymous, neither is His attitude and His law. God's character serves as the basis of His law, but the law does not encompass all that goes to make up His holy character. The Lord has tender feelings and emotions that cannot be expressed by law. Human laws serve as a framework for a judge to make a decision. And it is the duty of a judge to maintain the justice and integrity of the law. Yet in so doing, the judge sometimes has to make rulings that go against his or her own feelings and emotions. Thus it is with God.

This point is vital in understanding God's character in the context of the judgment. Although He is our endearing Father, He also presides as our Judge. And although the Son is our Advocate and Elder Brother, He will also act as Executor of justice when He comes the second time. We can see, then, why the Godhead is working overtime to persuade us to make the right decision. God wants us to choose aright so the processing of our case will be a joyful experience for everyone.

Yet, neither the Father nor the Son will force us. They can honor only the choices we make of our own free will. So by means of the judgment, as they determine before the universe exactly what choices we did make, and as they execute the results of those choices, we really judge ourselves. As free moral agents, our choice is an element and an issue in the judgement. But we must be careful not to make it the basis of our legal standing or of a positive outcome in the judgement. "In the work of redemption there is no compulsion. No external force is employed. Under the influence of the Spirit of God, man is left free to choose whom he will serve. . . . The expulsion of sin is the act of the soul itself" (*The Desire of Ages*, 466). If we are condemned in the end, it will not be because God arbitrarily condemned us. It will be because we condemned ourselves (see John 3:17-20).

The investigative judgment reveals the fact that God holds His creatures personally accountable for their choices and actions, just as do our earthly governments. Obedience to the laws of the land guarantees one's personal prosperity and freedom. Willful violation inevitably brings the transgressor to justice and strips him of his rights. Calvary granted us probationary freedom in which to exercise our spiritual right to choose, and the investigative judgment forever confirms our choice. It is the time when God eternally honors the decisions we have made in this life.

God desperately attempts to influence us to sign the peace accord between us and heaven. If we accept his offer of salvation, then He can use the merits of His saving blood to affirm our acquittal when our case goes to trial. In this way we can be found innocent in Him. But "there must be a forsaking of the sins the

Lord has reproved, before the soul can stand aquitted before God" (*Signs of the Times*, 13 December 1899). The "forsaking" spoken of here is in reference to our attitude toward sin. The statement is not saying we must literally get all sin out of our lives before we can have assurance of accquittal. It is speaking of a change of attitude and direction. Sorrow for our sins is the only evidence God can use before the jury of the universe to clear us, by His merits, of our crimes—and still remain just in doing so.

The judgment played out

Exactly how does God's justice system work in a practical sense?

Let's consider a sinner who is lost in sinful living. Through the divine influence, he makes a decision to comply with the conditions of God's plan to save him. Suppose this decision takes place on September 25, 1984. What has happened on that date? Well, that depends upon the genuineness of his experience. The moment he makes this decision, he is justified. The Scripture says, "If we confess our sins, he is faithful and just to forgive us our sins, and to cleanse us from all unrighteousness" (1 John 1:9). This means that the repentant sinner has received a "full, complete pardon of sin" (*The Faith I Live By*, 107). "Against his name on the balance sheet is written, Pardoned. Eternal Life" (*Our High Calling*, 53).

But, as we have seen earlier, although his sins have been pardoned, they are not removed from the books of record in the sanctuary above. "When sin has been repented of, confessed, and forsaken, then pardon is written against the sinner's name; *but his sins are not blotted out until after the investigative judgment*" (*Signs of the Times*, May 16, 1895, emphasis supplied). Although God knows whether a person's confession is true or not, "no finite being can tell how his case stands" (Ibid.). There-fore, there must be an investigative judgment to allow the inhabitants of the universe to see for themselves the genuineness of each profession.

Since God is omniscient, He could decide everyone's case without any investigation at all. But the stability of His government is based on the voluntary allegiance of all the citizens of the universe. They have a role in the stability of His government. He sees the necessity of His creatures being intimately involved in the affairs of the universe. Angels, we are told, have a part in the investigative judgment of human beings (see Daniel 7:9, 10). Redeemed humanity will also have a part in the millennial judgment of angels, which begins immediately after the second advent of Christ (see 1 Corinthians 6: 2, 3).

Many see an inconsistency between the fact that our sins remain on heaven's record books and God's promise that, at conversion, our sins are cast behind His back and into the depths of the sea (see Isaiah 38:17; Micah 7:19). But there is no inconsistency here. All sins, confessed and repented of, go beforehand to judgment (see 1 Timothy 5:24, 25). These will never be brought up for investigation in the judgment. They were as good as taken care of at the time of conversion. If we have Christ, then there is "no condemnation" and we "shall not come into condemnation" (Romans 8:1; John 5:24). If we are under His atoning blood, we are passed over in the time of judgment, just as the Hebrews were protected in Egypt when they put the blood on their doorposts. "For even Christ our passover is sacrificed for us" (1 Corinthians 5:7).

Also, although a person may have sincerely accepted Christ at the time of his conversion, his probation has not yet closed. At any time after conversion, this person has the right to reverse his decision and return to his former sins. If this is the case, it will not be because God went deep-sea fishing to retrieve his sins! The sinner did it of his own free will. The Bible says to turn our back on God and never come back, after having given ourselves to Him is worse than if we had never accepted

4—S.B.

the truth in the first place (see 2 Peter 2:20-22). "Be thou faithful unto death," the Bible urges, "and I will give thee a crown of life" (Revelation 2:10). "He that endureth to the end [in a relationship with Christ and keeping his eyes fixed on Him] shall be saved" (Matthew 10:22). But it also warns, "take heed unto yourselves, lest ye forget the covenant of the Lord your God, which He made with you" (Deuteronomy 4:23). "For if we sin wilfully after that we have received the knowledge of the truth, there remaineth no more sacrifice for sins" (Hebrews 10:26). This verse is not speaking of an occasional misdeed but of a determination to forget our relationship with Christ and continue to live our old selfish lives.

As long as the repentant sinner remains "in Christ," not willingly following a life of sinfulness and unbelief, his eternal well-being is secure. The sincerity of his profession is not determined by the "occasional good deeds and occasional misdeeds, but by the tendency of the habitual words and acts" (*Steps to Christ*, 58). It is really all about whether one is growing closer to the Lord or not. Then, when his name is called at the judgment, the Father will look to the Son. Jesus will raise His nail-pierced hands and cry, "My blood, Father; My blood!" Joyfully the Father will pronounce to the onlookers throughout the universe, "This case was settled out of court on September 24, 1984. Next name please!" At that time, the record of the reclaimed sinner's sins will be forever blotted from existence. They will be purged from the heavenly records without even being investigated at that time. The legal evidence that he truly accepted the saving grace of Christ will be his faithfulness to the covenant of grace throughout his probationary trial.

But what happens if the person willfully and intentionally resolves to leave Christ and breach the contract and covenant relation? In that case, when his name is called, the Father will look to Jesus, who with a saddened countenance will lower His head and begin to weep. The Father will then sadly and solemnly say, "We had better investigate this case more closely." As the books are brought forward, everyone will see exactly why. He has considered the world to be more valuable than his Savior and eternal life. If it is determined that everything that can be done for him has been done and that he has made his final decision, that person's name will be rejected before the universe. Only then will it be blotted out from the Lamb's book of life. And just think . . . God must live eternally with such decisions! With an eternal stare into the darkness, He will cry out in His great heart of love, "O my son Absalom, my son, my son Absalom! Would . . . I had died for thee, O Absalom, my son, my son" (2 Samuel 18:33).

Whatever the case, we may rest assured of one thing: The Lord will not allow any honest soul to be deceived by Satan's deceptive ways even "if every angel from heaven has to visit them, to enlighten their minds. We have nothing to fear in this matter" (*Testimonies for the Church*, vol. 1, 100). The only way souls will be lost is through their own persistent choice to be dishonest with God and themselves. They must allow themselves to be deceived by Satan's misconceptions about God and the sin problem.

Once all cases of the professed followers of Jesus are determined, the investigative phase of the judgment will come to a climactic close. Christ will stand up and make the solemn announcement, "He that is unjust, let him be unjust still: and he which is filthy, let him be filthy still: and he that is righteous, let him be righteous still: and he that is holy, let him be holy still. And, behold, I come quickly; and my reward is with me, to give every man according as his work shall be" (Revelation 22:11, 12). Then Jesus will exchange His priestly garments for kingly robes and lead the armies of heaven to the earth and physically redeem the saints who have passed the judgment *in Christ*. Those last two words need to be stressed. We do not pass the judgment on the basis of our behavior or obedience. We successfully pass the scrutiny of the judgment only because of our faith and trust in Christ's merits on our behalf.

Our Father recognizes that life is complex and that every case is unique. God deals with us in no rubber-stamp fashion. All the circumstances surrounding our lives—our genetic makeup, our birth, our home environment, our health, and our developing life experiences—all are delicately taken into consideration. Each of these factors will have its just weight in the final outcome of the judgment (see Psalm 87:6; *Testimonies for the Church*, 2:74). God "will have mercy." He is seeking to cover our sins whenever He legitimately can because we are in "a dispensation of mercy, not of rigid justice" (*The Youth's Instructor*, 27 August 1896). Yes, God is tenderly aware that the flesh is weak and remembers that we are dust. And He doesn't censure us for this (see *The Desire of Ages*, 689). It's all possible on account of our wonderful Savior and Substitute, Jesus Christ!

The boomerang effect

Before ending our look at the judgment, let's explore the logic of how the judgment relates to the golden rule.

The judgment is actually the flip side of the golden rule. Every thought, word, and action is like a boomerang that is sure to come back to us. Justice and judgment are simply the return swing of our own actions. "Be not deceived, God is not mocked, for whatsoever a man soweth, that shall he also reap" (Galatians 6:7). "For the day of the Lord is near upon all the heathen: as thou hast done, it shall be done unto thee: thy reward shall return upon thine own head" (Obadiah 1:15).

> "Judge not, that ye be not judged. For with what judgment ye judge, ye shall be judged: and with what measure ye mete, it shall be measured to you again." . . . The lesson contained in these words is of solemn import, and it is to be carefully considered. The law of the di-

vine government is that each one has the power of being the arbiter of his own destiny. What we do to others shall be done unto us again. Therefore we should be careful how we treat one another. We ever reap as we have sown, receiving back to ourselves what we have done to God and to our fellow-beings (*Review and Herald*, August 16, 1892).

We must realize that we have something coming back to us because of our hurtful, sinful behavior. What's more, we *must* meet these consequences unless we duck the boomerang and let it hit Christ. Actually, Jesus has already suffered the consequences of our sins on the cross, but we, personally, will not escape the retribution of our wrongs unless by faith we sprinkle our doorposts with the saving blood of "Christ our passover" (1 Corinthians 5:7). Only thus can we be set free from our deserved retribution.

Can you imagine Christ being judged in our place? Can you imagine Him feeling what every sinner has caused others to feel and experience? The guilt for billions of people and trillions of actions? Coupled with shame, embarrassment, and exposure before the universe as if He had been the source of all the problems sin has caused? Such was His experience on His cross. The retribution of our guilt and selfishness was the wrath of God that was poured out upon Him. The hiding of His Father's face meant that the covering of approval and innocence Christ deserved was withdrawn. He became the shameful outcast in our stead and was totally cut off from communion with God.

That was why, in comparison, His physical pain was hardly felt. Could it be that in the final judgment it won't be the cleansing fires that will deliver the most severe punishment to the wicked? Is it possible that the experience of graphically reliving in detail all the distress, pain, and suffering that we have inflicted on others and God (we are talking an eye for an eye and tooth for a tooth to the number and to the second) will be worse than the fire? Not to mention being exposed to open shame when all of our dark, devious thoughts and deeds are made apparent to the universe. Then on top of all this, it dawns upon our realization that there really was no legitimate reason for our conduct other than the persuit of our own selfishness. Could it be that this is how the justice side of the golden rule will be ultimately realized—when the guilty are made to feel the full guilt of their crimes?

Praise the Lord, there is a way to make certain that we never come into such a dreadful experience! It is God's intent and yearning hope for each of us that we opt to benefit from that boomerang bruising that Christ received in our stead. As Isaiah says, "Yet it pleased the Lord to bruise him; he hath put him to grief" (Isaiah 53:10). Oh, why shall we not shield ourselves from sin's awful return in judgment? God desperately desires to have us settle out of court now before it is forever too late.

Whenever we consider the investigative judgment, we need to keep all these things in perspective so we can avoid indifference toward this doctrinal pearl. And may we always remember the lesson our Lord taught when He said, "A bruised reed shall he not break, and smoking flax shall he not quench, till he *send forth judgment unto victory*" (Matthew 12:20, emphasis supplied). Without question, our poor carnal natures are like bruised reeds and smoking flaxes, with a strange beat that is prone to wander. But if, in faith, we battle against that gravitational pull away from God, and yield to the magnetic pull of Christ and His cross, then one day all our dreams will be realized in their fullest sense at the victory party on the sea of glass. Indeed, it is encouraging to know that it is our Father's good pleasure to give us the kingdom, and that judgment is to be in favor of the saints (see Luke 12:32; Daniel 7:22).

Investigating the Judgment—Part 2

Look upon Jesus, sinless is He; Father, impute His life unto me,

My life of scarlet, my sin and woe, Cover with His life, whiter than
snow

Deep are the wounds transgression has made; Red are the
stains, my soul is afraid,
O to be covered, Jesus with Thee, Safe from the law that now
judgeth me!

Longing the joy of pardon to know; Jesus holds out a robe white
as snow;
"Lord, I accept it! Leaving my own, Gladly I wear Thy pure life
alone."

Reconciled by His life (blood) for my sin, Justified by His life
pure and clean,
Sanctified by obeying His Word, Glorified when returneth my
Lord.

F. E. Belden

CHAPTER
10

The Righteousness of the Pharisees

In the great controversy, Satan has been successful in misrepresenting not only God's actions but those of His followers as well. The devil has the unusual ability to make those who keep God's law to appear as lawbreakers.

For example, take the incident recorded in Matthew 12:1-7. Jesus and His disciples were traveling through a field of grain on the Sabbath when the hungry disciples began to pluck heads of grain and eat. "But when the Pharisees saw it, they said unto him, Behold, thy disciples do that which is not lawful to do upon the sabbath day" (verse 2). Then, Jesus cited examples from the Old Testament to show that circumstances often change how the principles of the law are to be carried out in practical terms (see verses 3-5). In His disciples' defense, He stated a profound principle regarding how God views obedience to His law. He said to the Pharisees, "But if ye had known what this meaneth, I will have mercy, and not sacrifice, *ye would not have condemned the guiltless*" (verse 7, emphasis supplied).

Here we have opportunity to learn the most vital of all gospel lessons—how does one become righteous. The Pharisees believed that people become righteous by relating to the law of God in obedience. But here Jesus indicates that righteousness is obtained by God's mercy, not through sacrifice. Earlier, in His Sermon on the Mount, He had alluded to the Pharisees' misconception of what true righteousness really is. He told the people gathered there, "Except your righteousness shall exceed the righteousness of the scribes and Pharisees, ye shall in no case enter into the kingdom of heaven" (Matthew 5:20).

But in spite of such simple gospel teachings, the Pharisees' guidelines for securing righteousness through obedience continued to prevail in Judiasm. It also took strong root in the infant Christian church. In fact, it was this very point that produced so much confusion and contention among early Christian believers.

Initially the Christian church was primarily made up of two groups. First were the Hebrew Christians—Jews who had accepted Jesus as the Messiah. However, for the most part, they continued focusing on law keeping as a means of obtaining righteousness and acceptance with God.

Then there were the Gentile Christians. Though not blood descendants of Abraham, they had been grafted into God's church through the powerful preaching of the gospel after Pentecost. The Gentiles had experienced God's gift of righteousness, not through works but through their faith in what Christ had done in their behalf.

Understanding the primary differences between these two groups helps pinpoint the underlying reasons for the dissension among early church members.

Church headquarters were located in Jerusalem, giving the Jewish Christians a distinct advantage in terms of influencing the leadership of the church.

Then there was the apostle Paul. The majority of his labors were out in the mission field, away from church headquarters. I don't believe most Christians today truly understand just how radical Paul's commission was. This is perhaps because we do not usually consider it in the context of that time. His calling was to take the gospel to the Gentiles (see Acts 26). One would think the church members in Jerusalem would be elated to receive news of Paul's success among the heathen. But, most often, this was not the case. Reports of Paul baptizing people into Christ, without first circumcising them and indoctrinating them in other matters of Jewish law, caused an ever-growing concern among the Jewish segment of the church. Many feared that Paul, the very one God was using to deliver the true message of righteousness, was being used by the enemy to destroy the standards of Christianity.

It is no different in our day. The very ones God uses to deliver the true message of righteousness are often feared as the enemies of the faith. Because their focus does not center on law keeping and standards, they often appear as lawless "liberals" in the eyes of more conservative church members. People naturally assume they are only using the message of God's saving love as a smokescreen behind which they are attempting to dismantle God's law. This fear was the secret behind the devil's success in stifling the message of righteousness by faith as it was presented to Adventism in 1888.

But Paul was convinced in his own mind that righteousness was something that one received "by grace . . . through faith." He saw it as "the gift of God: not of works, lest any man should boast" (Ephesians 2:8, 9). He told the Galatians,

> Knowing that a man is not justified by the works of the law, but by the faith of Jesus Christ, even we have believed in Jesus Christ, . . . and not by the works of the law: for by the works of the law shall no flesh be justified (Galatians 2:16).

Yet the same apostle also taught the importance of obeying God through works (see Romans 1:5; Titus 1:16). He went on to teach the Galatians, "But if, while we seek to be justified by

Christ, we ourselves are found sinners, is therefore Christ the minister of sin? God forbid" (Galatians 2:17).

Here we see that Paul always maintained a healthy balance. Never did he lower the claims of God's law. Instead, he exalted the importance and the logical beauty of Jehovah's precepts. But Paul's secret to making the law attractive was to place it in a right relationship to the gospel of salvation by grace through faith. Many in his day made law keeping the condition of receiving eternal life, but the apostle showed that receiving salvation through God's grace was the only motivation for true obedience to the law.

Paul wrote earnestly to his Gentile converts about the traditional belief that righteousness was a state that could be achieved through law keeping. In Philippians 3, he warned them to "beware of evil workers" (verse 2). In the apostle's thinking, these evil workers were those who taught that righteousness was obtained by circumcision and the keeping of the law. Then he told the Philippian believers, "For we are the circumcision, which worship God in the spirit, and rejoice in Christ Jesus, and have no confidence in the flesh" (verse 3). The "flesh" referred to here is our human effort to obey God. In other words, Paul was teaching them not to have any confidence in how well they could keep the law in this mortal life.

Next, he gave his personal testimony of how diligently he had kept the law before knowing Christ. "As touching the law, [I was] a Pharisee; concerning zeal, persecuting the church; touching the righteousness which is in the law [righteousness that can be obtained by keeping the law], blameless" (verses 5, 6).

Note here the close correlation between the idea of righteousness by law keeping and the persecution of the church. Even today, there are those in Adventism who are not clear on this issue of how to fully attain to righteousness. To some degree, they still cling to the idea of keeping standards and obeying inspired counsels as their underlying hope of being made right with God. Though outwardly they often appear as defenders of the faith, eventually they end up turning against the main body of the church. Sooner or later they come to feel that the leadership of this movement is doing away with the historical truths of Adventism. This, in turn, leads them to become militant toward the church and to attempt to warn people of what they perceive to be apostasy.

But when Paul came to understand that no genuine righteousness can be obtained through the law but only through faith in what Jesus did for us on the cross, he counted the value of all the good things he had done as no more than a pile of rubbish (see verse 8). He then became an asset to the work of God's church and ceased to be an adder at its heels. From that time on, all Paul wanted was Jesus and to "be found in Him, not having mine own righteousness, which is of the law [the righteousness obtained through the keeping of the law], but that which is of the faith of Christ, the righteousness which is of God by faith" (verse 9).

Paul wrote a similar letter to the Roman believers in which he unloaded his burden that Israel was blinded by its own self righteousness. "What shall we say then?" he wrote. "That the Gentiles, which followed not after righteousness [who were not trying to become righteous through keeping the law], have attained to righteousness, even the righteousness which is of faith. But Israel, which followed after the law of righteousness [who were trying to become righteous through law keeping], hath not attained to the law of righteousness. Wherefore? [Why not?] Because they sought it [righteousness] *not by faith, but as it were by the works of the law*. For they stumbled at that stumblingstone [Christ]" (Romans 9:30-32 emphasis supplied).

The teaching of righteousness by faith alone lifts up the merits of Christ's life and His blood atonement as our only means of attaining to righteousness. To deny this fact by suggesting that our works in any way play a part in obtaining that righteousness is to deny the grace that Christ offers us. "Christ is become of no effect unto you, whosoever of you are justified by the law; ye are fallen from grace" (Galatians 5:4). Then Paul says, "For we through the Spirit wait for the hope of righteousness by faith" (verse 5). We must ever remember that it is righteousness by *faith*, not righteousness by *sight*. If we could realize righteousness through our visible works, then we would cease to hope for it because it would already be evident. "For we are saved by hope: but hope that is seen is not hope: for what a man seeth, why doth he yet hope for? But if we hope for that we see not, then do we with patience wait for it" (Romans 8:24, 25).

Paul poured out his heart's burden for Israel as he continued his letter to the Romans.

> Brethren, my heart's desire and prayer to God for Israel is, that they might be saved. For I bear them record that they have a zeal of God, but not according to knowledge. For they being ignorant of God's righteousness [which comes by grace through faith in Christ], and going about to establish their own righteousness [by keeping laws and standards], have not submitted themselves unto the righteousness of God. For Christ is the end of the law for righteousness to every one that believeth (Romans 10:1-4).

Much of the Christian world would suggest that when Paul wrote that "Christ is the end of the law for righteousness," he meant that a person is justified through faith in Christ, he is no longer under obligation to keep His law. But this false assumption is easily dispelled in the same epistle. Paul says clearly, "Do we then make void the law through faith? God forbid: yea, we establish the law" (Romans 3:31). We should never wrest Paul's letter to the Romans to mean that his emphasis on righteousness by faith is in any way lessening our duty to keep the law. In the very introduction of that letter he states that "we have received grace . . . *for obedience*" (Romans 1:5, emphasis supplied). Authentic faith will never lead us away from the desire to obey God's precepts. Rather, as James points out, faith always leads to good works (see James 2:21-23).

Yet in reading James, we must once again avoid the other ditch—that our works of obedience can in any way help justify us. Even though James seems on the surface to say this, such a concept is totally out of harmony with Scripture as a whole. The logical balance is that we are justified unto eternal life through faith, but that the works manifested in our life give evidence of our faith and will, in the end, determine whether or not our faith was genuine.

What did Paul mean, then, when he said that "Christ is the end of the law for righteousness to every one that believeth" (Romans 10:4). He simply meant that when one finds the righteousness that is available in Christ, it ends the attempt of trying to find righteousness through keeping of the law. Just as he says "Christ is the end [the purpose or goal] of the law *for righteousness.*" A radical shift is thus made in the believer's focus. His thoughts are no longer centered on what he can do to win God's favor but rather on what Christ has done to bring him into that favor.

That subject—what Christ has done in our behalf—will be the topic of the next chapter.

Rock of Ages, cleft for me, Let me hide myself in Thee;
Let the water and the blood, From Thy riven side which flowed,
Be of sin the double cure, Cleanse me from its guilt and power.

Not the labors of my hands, Can fulfill the law's demands;
Could my zeal no respite know, Could my tears forever flow,
All for sin could not atone, Thou must save, and Thou alone.

The Righteousness of the Pharisees

Nothing in my hand I bring, Simply to Thy cross I cling;
Naked, come to Thee for dress, Helpless, look to Thee for
grace,
Foul, I to the fountain fly; Wash me, Saviour, or I die.

When my pilgrimage I close, Victor o'er the last of foes,
When I soar to world's unknown, See Thee on Thy judgment
throne,
Rock of Ages, cleft for me, Let me hide myself in Thee.

Augustus M. Toplady

CHAPTER
11

Saved By Works?

Preachers are constantly looking for ways to get their congregations interested in the subject matter they wish to share. Good speakers know that a catchy introduction is vital if they hope to arrest the attention of their hearers and carry them into the sermon. Thus, as a speaker, I am constantly praying that the Lord will help me be creative in my public presentations.

Recently, He answered my prayer during a Sabbath morning service. As I introduced my subject, I decided to shake up everyone right at the beginning. I announced that as a result of nearly fourteen years of careful study of the Scriptures I had arrived at the profound conclusion that we are saved by works! Making sure that no one could misunderstand what I had said, I repeated what I had said. Then I paused to take inventory of people's facial expressions (as well as look for any flying objects!). Some people were smiling (either they hadn't read much of the Bible or they didn't care). Others were looking dumbfounded and scared (a this-guy-is-here-to-deceive-us type look). A few were most emphatically shaking their heads No! (I think I got their attention).

But I had my texts all ready and began to prove my point. What I presented that morning I would like now to share with you in this chapter. Now, before you put this book down (or burn it or whatever else you are thinking of doing), please give me the benefit of the doubt. I'm not quite as crazy as I might sound. What you are about to read is, in my opinion, revolutionary.

The gospel versus unbelief

We studied in our last chapter that "Christ is the end of the law for righteousness to every one that believeth" (Romans 10:4). As we realize the fact that it is impossible for our good deeds to make us righteous and that righteousness comes only by accepting Christ's righteousness in our behalf, we are led to rest in His merits. Then what Jesus said in Matthew 11:28 makes sense: "Come unto me all ye that labour [trying to become good enough for God] and are heavy laden, and I will give you rest."

Jesus invites us to enter into His rest, which is symbolized by the seventh-day Sabbath. Hebrews 4 is an explosive chapter of Scripture. As we begin associating righteousness by faith with the Sabbath, in the context of Hebrews 4, we will be able to proclaim the Sabbath "more fully" (*Early Writings*, 33). As a result, we will lead more people to keep the Sabbath than we have ever dreamed possible because the Sabbath will become a natural part of leading them to Jesus.

This is what God was attempting to do with ancient Israel during the wilderness wanderings. The record of Israel's experience provides the major context for Hebrews, chapters 3 and 4.

> But with whom was He [God] grieved forty years? Was it not with them that had sinned, whose carcases fell in the wilderness? And to whom sware He that they should not enter into His rest, but to them that believed not? So we see that they [Israel] could not enter in [to the promise of His rest] because of unbelief (Hebrews 3:17-19).

Here we are told what kept Israel out of the Promised Land. It was the sin of unbelief, not believing that what God was telling them through the gospel was true (Hebrews 4:1, 2).

The Lord had presented to Israel the same gospel of grace that He presents to us today (see Hebrews 4:2). He was trying to convince the Israelites that the only way they could find peace and rest was by relying on the work He would perform in their behalf. He promised to *give* them the land (see Numbers 13:2; 14:8), but they thought they had to take it by their *works*.

So it is with us today. Our greatest danger is in following "after the same example of unbelief" (Hebrews 4:11). Though God has promised to give us everlasting rest and peace through the gift of His righteousness, we, too, have been conditioned to think that we must do something to earn our eternal life. In this world, nothing comes free! Everything seems to have a catch to it. Smart people always read the fine print in order to discover the real agreement. So, this world has programmed us to look for the hook. Unfortunately, we apply the same skepticism toward God's offer of grace.

But God is not trying to hook any of us against our better judgment. Instead, He invites us to look His offer over. If we decide it's not for us, then that is our perogative. However, many throughout the course of this earth's history have found this gracious offer to be just what the Bible declares it to be—the best deal ever offered! And, it is available "without money and without price" (Isaiah 55:1).

Don't misunderstand. I still believe with all my mind that we are saved by works. But the works by which we are saved are not our works, but *the works of Christ*! Let me repeat that, so I won't be misunderstood. *We are saved by works—Christ's works, not ours.* Isaiah made this essential truth very plain when he said, "Lord, thou wilt ordain peace for us: for thou also hast wrought all our works in us" (Isaiah 26:12). In the King James Version of this text, the marginal reading for the phrase "in us" reads "for us." So the original reading of the text says, "Lord, Thou wilt ordain [establish] peace for us, for thou hast wrought [performed] all our works *for us*" (Ibid., emphasis supplied).

When was it that God performed those works for us? His "works were finished from the foundation of the world" (Hebrews 4:3). Before the foundation of the world was laid, the precious Lamb of God made the awesome decision to become our substitute and surety. In carrying out that decision, infinite wisdom performed the works of obedience that met the claims and demands of the law man transgressed. The real explosive truth of the gospel is that only Christ's obedient works can meet the claims of the broken law. Our personal acceptance of His substitutionary merits is the only way any of us can be made righteous before the universe.

When rightly understood, this truth will forever distinguish between the creature and his Creator. Christ declared that He came to "fulfil the law" (Matthew 5:17). We can keep God's law, but we can't fulfill it. Only Christ could fulfil, or satisfy, the demands of the broken law for us. Only Jesus could "fulfil all righteousness" (See Matthew 3:15). This truth is the dynamic power point of the doctrine of justification.

If you ask an Adventist what the phrase "under the law" means, he will tell you it means "under condemnation." But Galatians 4:21 says, "Tell me, ye that desire to be under the law . . ." So it doesn't make sense to substitute "under condemnation" for "under law." To do so would make Galatians 4:21 say, "Tell me, ye that desire to be under condemnation . . ."! The Judiazers did not practice circumcision or keep the Sabbath because they wanted to be condemned. No, they did it to be justified. "Under law" sometimes means using the law as a method of salvation. This, of course, is legalism. As long as we think we must fulfill the law as a condition of eternal life, we are "under the law." We have yet to come out of our pharisaical darkness and bask in the full "Sonshine" of the gospel. Of course, a believer keeps God's law, but he doesn't keep it to fulfill the terms of God's covenant. That is the work of the Mediator, the Lamb that was "slain from the foundation of the world" (Revelation 13:8).

This is the same point Ellen White was making when she wrote, "We cannot *perfectly* obey the holy law" (*Steps to Christ*, 62). We can obey it, but not perfectly enough to meets its demands. That's why Christ had to do it in our behalf. The Scriptures declare that Jesus was "made of a woman, made under the law" (Galatians 4:4).

But the gospel difference between Jesus being under the law and our being under the law is that His obedience to that law could form for Him a righteous character, whereas it cannot do the same for us because "we are sinful, unholy, [and] we cannot perfectly obey the holy law" (*Steps to Christ*, 62). Because of Jesus' perfect obedience to the law, He can legally count that obedience as our obedience on the condition of our willingness to accept it by faith. This is why Paul says that God's purpose for Jesus' perfect law keeping as a human was "to redeem them that were under the law" (Galatians 4:5).

So Christ did the work for us. In appreciation of this fact, He simply asks us to do good works for Him. "If ye love me," He said, "keep my commandments" (John 14:15). In no way do our works help produce our salvation. Instead, they are only the fruit of our salvation. Never should we think that our works help in our justification. This is unbelief. It's saying that Christ's substitutionary work was not good enough to satisfy the claims of the law. If we could meet the law's demands through our obedience, then we would'nt need Christ.

In this life, fallen creatures will never realize a state of inherent righteousness or sinlessness that is sufficient to meet the law's demands. Only the works of God in Christ from eternity past can accomplish that. This is one reason the gospel is called the "everlasting gospel," because it has been in existence from the foundation of the world. Such an obedience can be reached by the sinner only through faith in the fact that Christ obeyed for us and now offers His righteousness to us as a free gift. If this promise is accepted, then the sinner "stands in the sight of God uncondemned; for the righteousness of Christ is his: *Christ's perfect obedience is imputed to him*" (*Fundamentals of Christian Education*, 429, emphasis supplied). By faith, I must accept Christ's obedience in place of my own. This is the gospel. If it is not, then nothing is!

Does this mean, then, that our works are not important? What is the real purpose for our obedience to the Lord's revealed will?

Jesus told us the answer to that question in Matthew 5:16. He said, "Let your light so shine before men, that they may see your good works, and glorify your Father which is in heaven." Our works are simply for a witness to draw others to Christ that they may hear the good news of His gospel. Our good works don't make us holy. They don't make us righteous. They only make us a tool in God's hand to draw others to Himself.

Creature-oriented religion

Rightly understood, the gospel lays all human self-dependency in the dust. Because fallen humanity is creature oriented, it has a difficult time accepting this fact. The story of Paul and Barnabas when they visited the city of Lystra illustrates this. As the people there watched Paul healing a crippled man, they tried to worship him and Barnabas saying, "The gods are come down to us in the likeness of men" (Acts 14:11). But Paul reproved them by saying, "Sirs, why do ye these things? We also are men of like passions with you, and preach unto you that ye should turn from these vanities [worshiping the creature] unto the living God, which made heaven, and earth, and the sea, and all things that are therein" (verse 15; see also Revelation 14:7).

Fallen human nature hates this gospel that exposes its secret desire to be like God. This was shown in Lystra as the legalists, who were present that day, "persuaded the people" to stone Paul (verse 19). Just as Cain persecuted Abel and the Israelites turned on Caleb and Joshua, so will self-righteous men today persecute those who expose their legalistic religion through the preaching of the gospel. Isn't it strange how people can accept a god that they think is like them or one whom they feel they are capable of matching but get infuriated by the introduction of the God that is higher than heaven or earth?

The Lord plans that the gospel will be preached in all its fulness in these last days by men and women whom He has called into His service. In a world that still does not know God, can those who say, "Here am I; send me" (Isaiah 6:8) expect any different results than Paul and Barnabas experienced? But, as we enlist for the battle, we need to recall the words of our Commander, "Blessed are they which are persecuted *for righteousness sake*: for theirs is the kingdom of heaven" (Matthew 5:10, emphasis supplied).

This is the essence of the first angel's message. "And I saw another angel flying the midst of heaven, having the everlasting gospel [the good news of God's eternal works], . . . saying with a loud voice, Fear God and give glory to him; for the hour of his judgment is come" (Revelation 14:6, 7). The declaration of this angel is not about trying to live good enough to be found without spot or blemish before God's judgment seat. It is about accepting by faith His righteousness which is without spot or blemish.Only Jesus, through His substitutionary righteousness, can "present [us] faultless before the presence of his glory" (Jude 24). Only in this way can we "keep [but not fulfil] the commandments of God" and have "the faith of Jesus [a righteous standing through Him]" (see Revelation 14:12).

This message of justification by faith will lead us to examine seriously the real motives that prompt our obedience. That doctrine "is a discerner of the thoughts and intents of the heart"

(Hebrews 4:12). It tests the genuineness of our obedience by telling us that our works have no saving value before God. The saving power is in the blood of Christ! "When ye shall have done all those things which are commanded you, say, We are unprofitable servants: we have done that which was our duty to do" (Luke 17:10). God does not give us salvation because He owes it to us; rather, He provides it for us out of love. Any teaching that seeks to make God our debtor should be seen for its abhorrent content.

Unfortunately, this understanding sometimes causes those who have been inclined toward a religion of works to shift to a more liberal experience. For example, as the righteousness by faith message has been more openly declared in our churches, many have felt at liberty to put on jewelry, a practice that has never been sanctioned within Adventism. Though hardline conservatives tend to view such activity as apostasy, it is actually healthy because the message of freedom in Christ causes people to be honest with themselves, with others, and with God.

The heralding of the gospel helps reveal what has been in the heart all along. Instead of condemning those who desire to be openly honest, would it not be wiser to give each other space to balance out? If love for Christ truly dwells in our hearts by faith, it will eventually lead us back to obedience to all the standards of the Bible and for the right reason—love and respect for Christ. To continue with a religion that suppresses the real desires of the human heart just so everyone can appear holy on the outside only advances the devil's purposes in the church. But the preaching of the gospel here at the end of time is the very means by which God has designed to bring both wheat and tares to maturity.

God is seeking to purify the very source of all our actions— the motives. He desires genuine Christians. An apple tree does not bear apples in an attempt to be an apple tree. It bears apples *because* it is an apple tree. Likewise, true Christians don't obey in an attempt to be Christians. They bear the fruit of obedience *because*, by the grace of God, they are Christians.

With the true gospel, the law remains intact, yet it is no longer the focus of our attention. Instead, we become totally focused on Christ. Those who are "in Christ" do not have to be warned constantly against disobeying the law because now their greatest desire is to please God. In good marriages people go for decades without having to be reminded by their spouses not to commit adultery. It's the same with our relationship with God. If we are in a relationship of grace with Him, God doesn't have to be constantly bringing "thou shalt" and "thou shalt not" to our attention. Through Christ, we are "dead to the law" (Romans 7:4). The law speaks to those who are not yet under grace or to those who are in danger of departing from it (see Romans 3:19).

The true meaning of the Sabbath

The first earthly conflict between Cain and Abel was over justification. And the last religious conflict will be over justification as represented in the Sabbath issue which is symbolic of Christ's creative power and eternal work. The three angels' messages include both justification and Sabbath. One can be saved without the Sabbath, but no one can be saved without justification. The Sabbath doesn't bring salvation; justification does. The Sabbath reminds us of the righteous standing we lost at the Fall; justification gives it back again.

As the Jews failed to make the righteousness of Christ their own by faith, the Sabbath lost its true meaning to them. Satan was seeking to exalt himself through the creature and thus draw human beings away from Christ. He worked to pervert the Sabbath because it is the sign of Christ's power to save through justification (see Ezekiel 20:12). Those who so zealously claimed to keep the commandments of God and who were so jealous in honoring the Sabbath were the very ones who ended up crucifying the Lord of the Sabbath!

Seventh-day Adventists will be similarly deceived today unless we connect fully the doctrine of justification by faith to the Sabbath. The devil has a solid case against every one of us. Left to ourselves, we cannot refute his charges. This is why we must overcome him "by the blood of the Lamb" (Revelation 12:11). That blood is symbolic of His perfect, eternal performance that fully satisfies the penalty of the broken law. Thus we overcome by justification through Christ's life and death in our behalf.

We see, then, why the message of Christ's justifying blood is such a vital component to the "word of . . . [our] testimony [or evangelism]" (Revelation 12:11). It is what provides the third angel with his loud voice. The devil's whole program falls when confronted with the justifying blood of the Lamb. This is the atom bomb in the Christian's arsenal against sin and the devil. This is why Satan hates that message so much and the Sabbath that reveals it. It is the real reason behind why he used the little-horn power of Daniel's vision to substitute and cover up the justifying work of Christ with the sacraments of the papal religion (see Daniel, chapters 8 and 9).

Rome's usurpation of the Sabbath was merely the outward sign of its supposed authority to do away with the precious message of justification by grace through faith alone. Though the Protestant Reformers revived this great doctrine of justification by faith, they stopped short of connecting it with the law and the Sabbath. It was for this primary purpose that the Lord raised up Seventh-day Adventists here in the end of the world. We are to finish the reformation by connecting God's mercy and His justice—the message of righteousness by faith with His law (the Sabbath).

The Sabbath, when rightly understood, brings to view the finished work of God, both at Creation and at Calvary. Our work is never finished. Each week when the sun sets and the Sabbath begins, we put aside our unfinished work that we will again resume after the Sabbath is over. There is really never any true rest from our work. But it is not so with God.

At Creation, God created human beings on the sixth day. That means the first full day of Adam's and Eve's existence was spent resting on the Sabbath. I'm sure they wondered why the Lord told them to rest when they hadn't yet done anything. But that is exactly the point. Adam and Eve weren't resting from their works, but they joined God as He rested from His. So, from its very beginning, humanity has been given the invitation to reap the benefits of God's completed work.

The same was true at Calvary. When Jesus had finished doing everything that needed to be done in order to earn the right to be our saving Substitute, He said, "It is finished" (John 19:30). Then He died on that Friday afternoon and kept the Sabbath in the tomb. Now He invites each of us to enter into His rest. As we put aside our worldly labors each week and keep the Sabbath, *it is to be a reminder to us that God has done the work by which we are saved through justification.* There is nothing that anyone can add to, or take away from, what He did. And in case we forget this lesson, God has it come around to us every seventh day. "There remaineth therefore a rest [a Sabbath rest] to the people of God" (Hebrews 4:9).

This message is what brings true peace and rest to our souls. Without it, we shall ever be in turmoil. The problem with the wicked at the end of time is that they have no rest. "And the smoke of their torment ascendeth up for ever and ever: and they have no rest day nor night, who worship the beast and his image, and whosoever receiveth the mark of his name" (Revelation 14:11). "Peace, peace to him that is far off, and to him that is near, saith the Lord; and I will heal him. But the wicked are like the troubled sea, when it cannot rest, whose waters cast up mire and dirt. There is no peace, saith my God, to the wicked" (Isaiah 57:19-21).

Saved By Works?

May God help each of us learn what Israel refused to learn, "For thus saith the Lord God, the Holy One of Israel: In returning and rest shall ye be saved; in quietness and in confidence [in Christ's merits to save us] shall be your strength" (Isaiah 30:15).

Come every soul by sin oppressed, There's mercy with the
Lord;
And He will surely give you rest, By trusting in His Word.

For Jesus shed His precious blood, Rich blessings to bestow;
Plunge now into the crimson flood, That washes white as snow.

Yes, Jesus is the truth, the way, That leads you into rest;
Believe in Him without delay, And you are fully blest.

Come, then, and join this holy band, And on to glory go,
To dwell in that celestial land, Where joys immortal flow.

Only trust Him, only trust Him, Only trust Him now;
He will save you, He will save you, He will save you now.

J. H. Stockton

CHAPTER
12

The Alpha and Omega of Apostasies

Back in the first chapter of this book we examined the warfare that began in heaven with the angel Lucifer over God's governing principles. This warfare we identified as the great controversy.

But the great controversy is not the major theme of the Scriptures. The grand message of the Bible is God's love for His fallen creatures and the merciful plan He has designed to save them. The great controversy is simply the dark side of the plan of salvation. It reveals how the forces of evil are attempting to thwart God's saving purposes on the earth.

In reviewing the fall of angels and humanity, we see the introduction of a science called "pantheism." Pantheism is composed of spiritualistic theories that appear to be beautiful, truthful, and uplifting. Its end result, however, is to confuse the creature's mind so that it is unable to clearly distinguish the relationship between the creature and his Creator.

In reference to the initial fall into sin by one of God's creation, the Bible asks the question, "How art thou fallen from heaven, O Lucifer, son of the morning?" (Isaiah14:12). Through Isaiah, the Lord goes on to answer this initial question as to how Lucifer fell from his holy state. He says, "For thou hast said in thine heart, . . . I will be like the most High" (verses 13, 14). This was the true alpha of apostasy. Through pantheism, Lucifer, a created being, became confused and lost the ability to distinguish clearly between himself and his Creator. He came to view God as a Being like himself and thought he could become inherently holy like God.

For a creature to think that he can become "like" God in the sense that he can equal God's spiritual state of being is like the moon thinking it can become the sun. The moon has no inherent light of its own but receives its every ray from the sun. Though it can reflect what light the sun sends its way, the moon can never, ever, be the sun.

So it is in the creature's relationship to God. The creature can reflect whatever light God sends its way, but created beings can never be "like" God in the fullest sense of the word. By failing to accept this fact, Lucifer was led to consider the impossible. The more he entertained the thought of becoming like God, the less impossible it seemed. Imperceptibly his mind was being weakened, although he imagined he was achieving a higher plane of spirituality.

The devil has successfully employed this same science in his campaign to "weaken the nations" on the earth (Isaiah 14:12). He told Eve that if she and her husband would simply follow his instruction and disobey God, then "your eyes shall be opened, and ye shall be as gods" (Genesis 3:5). We have been given insight into the experience Eve had as she adopted this pantheistic concept. "She then plucked for herself of the fruit and ate, and imagined she felt the quickening power of a new and elevated existence as the result of the exhilarating influence of the forbidden fruit" (*The Spirit of Prophecy*, 1:38).

But Satan's use of pantheistic science did not cease at the Garden of Eden. Every major world religion holds some spiritualistic theory at it's theological core. Such have been "elated with their ideas of progression and charmed with their own vain philosophy, but grope in midnight darkness relative to true knowledge. They are ever learning and never able to come to the knowledge of the truth" (*Lift Him Up*, 21).

The apostle Paul also wrote about such a class in his letter to the Romans. He said, "When they knew God, they glorified him not as God, neither were thankful; but became vain in their imaginations [their mental conception of the nature of God], and their foolish heart was darkened. Professing themselves to be wise, they became fools, and changed the glory of the uncorruptible God into an image made like to corruptible man [their mental perception of what God was like], and to birds, and fourfooted beasts, and creeping things. . . Who changed the truth of [about] God into a lie, and worshipped and served the creature more than the Creator, who is blessed for ever" (Romans 1:21-25).

Here is the underlying principle behind all false religious theories. It leads one to focus more on the spiritual advancement of the creature rather than on God. By this means the fallen creature attempts to forget his accountability to his Creator while still maintaining a semblance of reverence toward Him. This form of godliness serves only to satisfy his inherent need to worship. That's why Jesus said, "Ye worship ye know not what" (John 4:22). Pantheism leads us to believe that we are really worshiping God in truth, when in reality we are worshiping ourselves in a lie.

This was the major principle behind the introduction of the pagan Sunday into the worship of the Christian church. That day has only the authority of the creature behind its supposed holiness. And who was it that instituted and has propagated that practice throughout the world? It was "that man of sin . . . , the son of perdition; who opposeth and exalteth himself above all that is called God, or that is worshipped; so that he as God sitteth in the temple of God, shewing himself that he is God" (2 Thessalonians 2:3, 4).

As a result, there are only two types of world religion here at the end of time. One is the true religion of God as revealed through the Bible. The other, which embraces all the false religions of the world, is based on the erroneous doctrines and traditions of mankind which teach that human beings can help save themselves and eventually become "as gods." The true purpose of Seventh-day Adventism is to help the inhabitants of the earth to clearly distinguish between these two.

But Satan has also made inroads into the remnant church in his attempt to spiritually confuse those to whom God has entrusted the three angels' messages. Though it is hard on our pride to admit it, pantheism has been incorporated into several traditional teachings within Adventism. These errors have been held by successive generations down through the history of our movement. Yet, at each step God has had His chosen ones on hand to refute these unbiblical teachings.

It is going to be an intense struggle for the members of this church to sort out this erroneous chaff from the wheat here at the end of time. Nevertheless, it must be done.

Pantheism among the pioneers

Patheism posed a serious threat to the life and mission of the church at the beginning of the twentieth century. It was then that Dr. John Harvey Kellogg began to openly promote dangerous pantheistic views through his book *The Living Temple*. In that book, he presented perverted views concerning the relationship between God and His creation.

If accepted and allowed to fully develop, these views would have undermined the theological pillars of our faith and led to the downfall of the church. The Lord showed Ellen White the dangerous nature of Kellogg's teachings and directed her to meet it publicly. Thus, the church was saved from fatal deception in 1903.

But this was not to be the last time the deadly science of pantheism would threaten the security and spiritual prosperity of God's remnant people. Speaking of the effect that this planted seed of pantheism would one day bear in our church, Ellen White wrote,

> Be not deceived; many will depart from the faith, giving heed to seducing spirits and doctrines of devils. We have now before us the alpha of this danger. The omega will be of a most startling nature. . . . In the book *Living Temple* there is presented the alpha of deadly heresies. The omega will follow, *and will be received by those who are not willing to heed the warning God has given* (*Selected Messages*, bk. 1, 197, 200, emphasis supplied).

Many have been the attempts, since this counsel was written, to identify exactly what the omega of apostasy will be. We need to be careful in trying to identify with certainty exactly what Ellen White was talking about. History has revealed that whenever one goes so far as to think that he knows precisely what the apostasy is, he ends up being the next apostate. The best that we can do is to speculate as to what it might be. The extent and strength of its influence within the church will be realized only as it is played out before us.

However, we can historically trace some of the impact that this "alpha of deadly heresies" has made within the theological circles of our denomination. So now let us examine in the light of God's holy Scriptures these seducing spirits and doctrines of devils.

My faith has found a resting place, Not in a man-made creed;
I trust the ever living One, That He for me will plead.

Enough for me that Jesus saves, This ends my fear and doubt;
A sinful soul I come to Him, He will not cast me out.

The Alpha and Omega of Apostasies

My soul is resting on the Word, The living Word of God:
Salvation in my Savior's name, Salvation through His blood.

The great Physician heals the sick, The lost He came to save;
For me His precious blood He shed, For me His life He gave.

I need no other evidence, I need no other plea;
It is enough that Jesus died, And rose again for me.

Lidie H. Edmunds

CHAPTER
13

Seducing Spirits and Doctrines of Devils— Part 1

We have already defined pantheism as the false science that views God as synonymous with His creation. J. H. Kellogg taught that God was inherently present in the things of nature, such as the flowers and trees. In succeeding years, prominent teachers within Adventism would go on to promote this same concept by teaching that God was literally present in human beings themselves.

Such theological views, identifying God with fallen man, have been perpetuated through the years within the church. Even today, some proclaim these ideas to be authentic teachings of Seventh-day Adventism. Yet, when placed side by side with truth, the pantheistic nature of these teachings are seen to blur the distinction between us as created beings and our Creator.

The humanity of Christ

From its beginning, our church struggled with Arian beliefs concerning the nature of Christ's divinity before He became a human being. Arianism denied the preexistence of Christ prior to His birth in Bethlehem. However, by the early 1930s the church unanimously came to agree that Jesus was indeed a preexistent, eternal member of the Godhead.

While the church's understanding of Christ's preexistence before Bethlehem was being worked out, Elders A. T. Jones and E. J. Waggoner opened up a whole new field of debate—what kind of human nature did Christ possess? The arguments they presented have extended all the way down to our present day.

At the 1895 General Conference, Jones presented the thought that there was *"not a particle of difference"* between Christ's human nature and ours. He believed that in order for Jesus to qualify as our Savior He had to have the identical fallen nature that we received from Adam. Only thus, according to Jones, could Jesus be our example in overcoming the trials that beset humanity.

But Jones's statement, that there was not a particle of difference between Christ's human nature and our own, immediately conflicted with a statement Ellen White had written just five years earlier. "He [Christ] had not taken on Him even the nature of angels, but humanity, *perfectly identical with our own nature, except without the taint of sin.* . . . Christ took our nature, *fallen but not corrupted*, and would not be corrupted unless He received the words of Satan in the place of the words of God" (*Manuscript Releases,* 16:180, 181, 183, emphasis supplied). The human nature we receive at birth is both fallen and corrupted. But notice that although the human nature Jesus inherited was fallen, it was not corrupted. If His nature had been "perfectly identical" with ours, as Jones had taught, then the word *except* is out of place in Sister White's declaration.

"At it's very source [Adam's sin] human nature was corrupted" (*Review and Herald*, 16 April 1901). Adam corrupted his nature through self-seeking. He then passed that nature on to all his offspring. Thus "selfishness is inwrought in our very being. It has come to us as an inheritance" (HS, 138, 139). But "Christ did not possess the same sinful, corrupt, fallen disloyalty we possess" (*Selected Messages*, bk.3, 131). Clearly, Jesus was not exactly like us in terms of His human heredity. These, and other inspired statements, point out the false assumption made by Jones in 1895.

Adam was in harmony with God when he was created. But after he sinned, "his heart was at war with the principles of God's law" (*The Great Controversy*, 467). Ever since, the human race has possessed an "enmity against God" (Romans 8:7). "Enmity against Satan is not natural to the human heart; it is implanted by the grace of God" (*The Desire of Ages*, 407). We are not born with enmity against Satan and sin. It can be obtained only through grace. In honor of our own decision to serve Him, God begins implanting that enmity into our natures by writing His law in our hearts (see Hebrews 10:16).

Yet this is not how it was with Jesus. He came into this world inherently possessing enmity against sin and Satan. Prophesying of Jesus' first advent, the psalmist wrote, "Then said I, Lo, I come: in the volume of the book it is written of me, I delight to do thy will, O my God: yea, *thy law is within my heart*" (Psalm 40:8, emphasis supplied). Concerning Jesus, "the enmity [against sin] was in one sense natural" (*Selected Messages*, bk. 1, 254). With us, love for God's law and hatred toward sin never comes naturally.

In all points . . .

Some teach that Christ possessed the corruptions and tendencies of the carnal nature. They quote Hebrews 4:15, "For we have not an high priest which cannot be touched with the feeling of our infirmities; but was in all points tempted like as we are, yet without sin." This they interpret to mean that He struggled with and overcame the identical sinful tendencies that we do. Thus He is thought of as a perfect example for us in our struggle to overcome our natural defects.

Without question, He is our perfect example of how we are to overcome in that fight against our human bent toward sin. But was His struggle necessarily identical with ours?

The apostle John told us, "Love not the world, neither the things that are in the world. . . for all that is in the world, the lust of the flesh, and the lust of the eyes, and the pride of life, is not of the Father, but is of the world" (1 John 2:15, 16). Here John brings to view the three avenues by which every temptation presents itself to humanity. But this doesn't necessarily mean that everyone is tempted in exactly the same manner. "Every man is tempted, when he is drawn away of his own lust, and enticed" (James 1:14). The lust that entices you may not be the lust that entices me. Your weakness on a certain article of food, for example, may not be my identical weakness, and mine may not be yours. Yet we both are tempted on the point of appetite. When it comes to designing temptations, the devil is an expert tailor. He can design a custom fit for everyone.

So it was with the temptations presented to Jesus. In the wilderness of sin He was indeed "in all points tempted like as we are, yet without sin" (Hebrews 4:15). When He fasted forty days, He was as hungry as you or I would have been. Yet, when it came time for His temptation on the point of appetite, we don't see Satan pulling up in a Domino's delivery truck trying to get Him to indulge in a hot pepperoni pizza, along with a mug of beer. That might be tempting to some people but not to our Lord. It was wholesome bread, probably Jewish rye, that Satan used to tempt Jesus.

But the real nature of the temptation wasn't eating bread. The real temptation for Jesus was to use His divine power to release Himself from the tight spot in which His humanity had placed Him. "If thou be the Son of God, command that these stones be made bread" (Matthew 4:3). If Christ had done that, then He would have done something that is impossible for us to do—use inherent divinity to overcome human tendencies. He would have thereby failed in providing us an example of how we can overcome. But He resisted this first temptation by relying on the divine power of His Father in heaven to make a way of escape for Him.

We can, and must, overcome tempatation in the same way. "There hath no temptation taken you but such as is common to man: but God is faithful, who will not suffer [allow] you to be tempted above that ye are able; but will with the temptation also make a way to escape, that ye may be able to bear it" (1 Corinthians 10:13). Because of our sinful human natures, you and I have the tendency to gravitate toward the sinful and the common, back to the vomit and the mire (see 2 Peter 2:22) when we get in a tight spot.

With Jesus it was the exact opposite. His greatest temptation was to use a little of His divine power in His own behalf. As we resist this gravitational pull of our sinful natures and rely, as Jesus did, on our heavenly Father to deliver us from temptation, we are overcoming the same way He did.

When the devil took Jesus to the top of the temple, he tempted Him with the "pride of life" (Matthew 4:5,6). He insinuated that if Jesus really was the Son of God, He needed to prove His importance. How often we try to do just that very thing, even though we would never consider jumping off a building. The devil tempts us to place too high an estimate on ourselves. Or he tries to get us to think of ourselves as worthless. Both are extreme attitudes that stem from the "pride of life." Such moral deficiency can be cured only through finding our true self-worth in the light of God's love for us.

And when the devil appealed to the "lust of the eyes" (Matthew 4:8,9), He didn't show Jesus the red light district of Tokyo or Times Square in New York City. We are plainly told what he presented to the Savior's view. "Satan caused the kingdoms of the world, in all their glory, to pass in panoramic view before Him. The sunlight lay on templed cities, marbled palaces, fertile fields, and fruit-laden vineyards. The traces of evil were hidden. The eyes of Jesus, so lately greeted by gloom and desolation, now gazed upon a scene of unsurpassed lovliness and prosperity" (*The Desire of Ages*, 129). Notice, Satan had to hide all traces of evil in order to make the temptation attractive to Jesus! To carnal men, it is the evil that draws them.

All the way to the cross such temptations assailed our Savior. Even at Calvary we hear the devil still tempting Him in the voices of His critics: "He saved others; let him save himself, *if he be Christ*, the chosen of God" (Luke 23:35, emphasis supplied). Think of it! At any moment Jesus could have pushed the red button of destruction on the devil and this fallen world. I know one thing—if I had the power to do that, the devil would have been history a long time ago! Yet, if Jesus had destroyed Satan, the plan of salvation would have failed. Therefore, because of the love He had for His fallen creatures, Jesus "resisted unto blood," refusing to use divinity in His own behalf (see Hebrews 12:4). His nature was, and still is, bent on saving every single soul He can.

A virgin shall conceive

Inspiration also tells us that "as the sinless One, His [Jesus'] nature recoiled from evil" (*Testimonies for the Church*, 2: 202). Does that sound like an accurate description of our human natures? The glory of Christ's incarnation can best be realized not by focusing so much on how He was made *like* us. Rather, by discovering the ways in which He *differed* from us we will better discern "the light of the knowledge of the glory of God in the face of Jesus Christ" (2 Corinthians 4: 6). Jesus is the windowpane through which we view God. He Himself said, "He that hath seen me hath seen the Father" (John 14:9). Our understanding of what Jesus is like is exactly what we understand God to be like. Only through a balanced view of His humanity shall we clearly distinguish His divinity. Then we shall better realize who He really was—God incarnated in human flesh!

Indeed, Jesus accepted the working of human genetics. His mother was a human who possessed a fallen nature. This is why He was physically and mentally weakened by 4,000 years of sin.

We see this in the fact that He got hungry, thirsty, tired, and sorrowful. His stature and vital force were not like those of Adam as he came from the Creator's hand. Nor did Christ's mind possess the power of prefallen humanity. The Creation had been established by His own power, but in His humanity He had to learn all about it from lessons at His mother's knee.

Regarding the spiritual nature Jesus possessed as a human, Ellen White wrote, "His spiritual nature was free from every taint of sin" (*Signs of the Times*, 9 December 1897). That was because His genetic Father was not a fallen human being. For Him, Papa was an unfallen God! Simple logic should tell us this fact alone rendered it impossible for Him to have been totally identical to us. When my father used to cross-breed cattle, we never expected to see calves totally identical to just one parent. So when it comes to the greatest conception that was ever to take place, why would we think that Jesus would be perfectly identical to His mother's side of the family? Did He not have a more potent genetic factor involved in His conception?

Obviously, God allowed the fallen genes to have some bearing on Jesus' physical and mental condition. But when human genetics tried to interfere with His spiritual nature, Divinity said No! Christ's spiritual composition was holy ground, upon which the depraved heredity of sin was forbidden to enter. This had to be, for He was to be called "that holy thing" (Luke 1:35). As the apostle later wrote concerning Him, "For such an high priest became us, who is *holy, harmless, undefiled, separate from sinners*, and made higher than the heavens" (Hebrews 7:26, emphasis supplied).

Because Jesus was not exactly like us, His experience in a sinful enviroment would naturally be drastically different from ours. Notice: "It was as difficult for Him to keep the level of humanity as for men to rise above the low level of their depraved natures, and be partakers of the divine nature" (*SDA Bible Commentary*, 7:930). Once again, with us the struggle is to suppress the corrupt clamorings that stem from our fallen, carnal natures.

But for Jesus, the struggle was to maintain His choice to remain incarnate in humanity amid a hostile and distasteful society. This was due to the fact that "as the sinless One, His nature recoiled from evil" (*Testimonies for the Church*, 2:202).

It would be somewhat like taking a seventy-eight-year-old Adventist grandmother—someone who had never once cursed or drank alcohol or smoked a cigarette or even eaten a piece of meat in her entire life—to a worldly drug party on Friday night! Imagine dropping that soul off, as the Sabbath hours began, at a house where the night was to be spent in drunken revelry and sexual perversities. As you let the dear lady out, you tell her to give you a call the moment she feels like coming home! How long do you suppose she would want to stay?

That is something of what it was like for Jesus to be in our world in human nature—except that, for Him, sin's offensive nature was infinitely intensified because of His holy nature. At any time He could have checked out of the party down here by deciding to return to His preincarnate state. It would have been so easy for Him to let humanity pay for its own sins. But out of love for us who were helpless to wriggle away from sin's ensnaring grasp, He subjected Himself for over thirty years to the abusive and disgusting presence of sin. He stayed committed to His holy purpose unto the end, "even [to] the death of the cross" (Philippians 2:8). Thus He spoke truth to the Pharisees when He said, "Ye are from beneath; I am from above: ye are of this world; I am not of this world" (John 8:23).

A righteous substitute

It is important to understand that Jesus did not have to be just like us in every way in order to be our Savior. In fact, if He had been exactly like us, He would have automatically been disqualified to be our Redeemer. This sublime fact is made clear in the following statement: "It was possible for Adam, *before the fall, to form a righteous character* by obedience to God's law.

But he failed to do this, and *because of his sin our natures are fallen and we cannot make ourselves righteous* [by obedience to God's law]. Since we are sinful, unholy, we cannot perfectly obey the holy law" (*Steps to Christ*, 62, emphasis supplied).

Because of Adam's sin, each of us has been placed in a position whereby our obedience to God's law, on its own merit, *cannot* form for us a righteous character. This is why a legal approach to character perfection is futile." Christ revealed an *infinitely perfect character*" (*Testimonies for the Church*, 6:60, emphasis supplied). We all need the righteous character that Christ wrought out in His humanity if we ever hope to be considered righteous before the eyes of the universe.

So, if Jesus had received from Adam the same sinful nature we do, then how could His obedience to the law have formed for Him a righteous character to be offered in our behalf? He, like us, would not have been able to perfectly obey the holy law. He, Himself, would have needed a Savior. The idea that Jesus was just like us, although it may sound reasonable on the surface, subtly undermines the doctrine of righteousness by faith.

The teaching that Christ inherited the identical, sinful nature that we do is actually a creation of the carnal mind itself. "The heart in love with sin clothe[s] Him [God] with its own attributes, and this conception strengthen[s] the power of sin. Bent on self-pleasing, men came to regard God as such a one as themselves" (*Education*, 75).

This teaching suggests that God, as viewed through Christ, is selfish by nature. This is the identical charge Satan made before the universe in the courts of heaven (see *The Desire of Ages*, 57). And the devil hasn't changed his mind about Christ. Through men, well meaning though they be, he continues to spew out His blasphemy.

But the Lord has promised that He will clarify this issue in our minds. After identifying the sins resulting from Israel's corrupt nature, He went on to say, "These things you have done, and I kept silent; you thought I was altogether like you. But I will rebuke you and accuse you to your face" (Psalm 50:21,NIV). We cannot get a clear view of our sinful nature until we see it in contrast to the purity of Jesus' holy life. That life, without His atoning death, would only have condemned us. This is why we fallen creatures can bear the contemplation of His holy nature only as we behold it through the saving blood of His cross.

He who knew no sin

But there is also a danger in failing to realize that in His humanity Jesus actually experienced the most degraded existence to which any person has ever fallen. "He took upon Himself fallen, suffering human nature, degraded and defiled by sin" (*SDA Bible Commentary*, 4:1147). The Bible clearly teaches that when Jesus went to the cross, He took humankind's perverted nature with Him and nailed it there to His cross. "Knowing this, that our old man is crucified with him, that the body of sin might be destroyed, that henceforth we should not serve sin" (Romans 6:6).

"But," someone says, "I thought we just learned that Jesus didn't have our sinful, human nature? If so, how could He have taken it to the cross with Him? Why would Ellen White say in one place that He 'did not possess the same sinful, corrupt, fallen disloyalty we possess' and then turn right around in another place and state that 'He took upon Himself fallen, suffering human nature, degraded and defiled by sin' " (compare *Selected Messages*, bk. 3, 131 with *SDA Bible Commentary*, 4:1147)? Such apparently conflicting statements have been the root cause of many a debate on this subject between Adventists over the years.

In fact, Ellen White makes several statements regarding Christ's human nature that seem contradictory. Let's consider a few:

- "In him was no guile or sinfulness; he was ever pure and undefiled, yet he took upon him our sinful nature" (*Review and Herald*, December 15, 1900).

- "He took upon His sinless nature our sinful nature, that He might know how to succor those that are tempted" (*Medical Ministry*, 181).
- "Christ did in reality unite the offending nature of man with his own sinless nature" (*Review and Herald*, July 17, 1900).

The answer to this perplexity is found in the earthly sanctuary service of the Old Testament. The sacrificial lamb was to be perfect, without spot or blemish. As it was brought to the sanctuary, the contaminating guilt of the sins committed by the sinner was transferred to that innocent creature. Though inherently free itself from any defilement of sin, the lamb became defiled by serving as a substitute for the guilt-ridden, sin-depraved confessor.

Of course, we know that the lamb was a representation of the great Lamb of God, which was to take away the sins of the world. Just as the ceremonial lamb was free from any defilement of its own, so Jesus entered this earth with a nature that was sinless. But when He actually became the substitute for the sins of mankind, He became defiled by those sins. "For he [the Father]hath made him [Jesus Christ] *to be sin for us, who knew no sin*; that we might be made the righteousness of God in him" (2 Corinthians 5:21, emphasis supplied). In this way, He took "upon His sinless nature [the one He received when He came into this world] our sinful nature [the one we transferred to Him as our substitute]." (*Medical Ministry*, 181). He "united the offending nature of man [the one He received by substitution] with His own sinless nature [the one He inherently received at His birth]" *Review and Herald*, July 17, 1900).

But exactly when did Jesus go through this process of uniting our defiled nature to His spotless and pure nature? Ellen White brings to light that there were several times during Christ's ministry that He experienced, in limited degrees, the terrible weight of the guilt of this world's sins—when He was in the wilderness of temptation and at Gethsemane. Yet these were but a sample of what He would ultimately go through at Calvary. It was there that "the Lord laid on Him the iniquity of us all." It was on Golgotha that He was brought "as a lamb to the slaughter." It was when they cut His flesh that "he was cut off out of the land of the living" (Isaiah 53:6-8). It was there on that old rugged cross that our Savior, our precious innocent Savior, actually bore "our griefs and carried our sorrows" to their awful, deadly conclusion (see verse 4).

All through His earthly life Jesus gained strength and courage as He sensed the approval of His heavenly Father. To hear those words, "This is my beloved Son, in whom I am well pleased" (Matthew 3:17), meant more to Him than life itself. It was the realization of the Father's favor and acceptance that had gotten Him through His difficult experience of being in a world that repudiated Him. But speaking of that night in Gethsemane, as Jesus was approaching the shadow of the cross, Ellen White wrote, "Christ was now standing in a different attitude from that which He had ever stood before. . . . The sins of men weighed heavily upon Christ, and the sense of God's wrath against sin was crushing out His life" (*The Desire of Ages*, 686, 687). We need to recognize that God's wrath was not turned upon Jesus because of any inherent sin in His own nature. "It was the sense of sin, bringing the Father's wrath upon Him *as man's substitute,* that made the cup He drank so bitter, and broke the heart of the Son of God" (Ibid., 753, emphasis supplied).

It was at Calvary that Jesus most closely identified with those He came to save. What really transpired there will forever be a mystery. It will take eternity and beyond to comprehend how Jesus actually became identified with the kingdom of sin in our behalf. Yet we can be assured that it was the most difficult thing He ever did, because "Satan told Him that if He became the surety for a sinful world, the separation [from His Father] would be eternal. He would be identified with Satan's kingdom, and would nevermore be one with God" (*The Desire of Ages*, 687).

Through inspiration we have been provided with this incredible account of the time when our sacrificing God most closely identified Himself with the experience of His lost creatures. "In His closing hours, while hanging upon the cross, *He experienced to the fullest extent what man must experience when striving against sin*. He realized how bad a man may become by yielding to sin. He realized the terrible consequences [guilt] of the transgression of God's law; for the iniquity of the whole world was upon Him" (*SDA Bible* Commentary, 5:1082).

"Behold, a virgin shall conceive, and bear a son, and shall call his name Immanuel" (Isaiah 7:14). This is our God who came to be with us!

On a hill far away stood an old rugged cross,
The emblem of suffering and shame,
And I love that old cross where the dearest and best
For a world of lost sinners was slain.

Oh, that old rugged cross, so despised by the world,
Has a woundrous attraction for me,
For the dear Lamb of God left His glory above,
To bear it to dark Calvary.

In the old rugged cross, stained with blood so divine,
A woundrous beauty I see.
For 'twas on that old cross Jesus suffered and died
To pardon and sanctify me.
So I'll cherish the old rugged cross,
Till my trophies at last I lay down;
I will cling to the old rugged cross,
And exchange it some day for a crown.
—George Bennard

CHAPTER
14

Seducing Spirits and Doctrines of Devils— Part 2

The Bible declares, "The just shall live by faith" (Romans 1:17). The writer of Hebrews equates faith with believing in God. He says, "Without faith it is impossible to please him [God]: for he that cometh to God must believe that he is, and that he is a rewarder of them that diligently seek Him" (Hebrews 11:6). There have ever been two conflicting stories regarding the great controversy—God's story and Satan's. It is up to us to choose whom we are going to believe. And our experience will reflect that choice, because our actions are an accurate barometer of our faith.

For example, we know that Eve believed Satan, because she indulged in the forbidden fruit. And today the devil is still tempting us to "depart from the faith [belief in the sufficiency of Christ's saving blood atonement in our behalf], giving heed to seducing spirits, and doctrines of devils" (1 Timothy 4:1). Though these lies be clothed with a semblance of traditional holiness, if accepted as truth, they will end up playing havoc with our faith.

One such false concept is the doctrine of extreme sanctification. In the last chapter we examined the teaching that Christ's humanity is identical to our fallen human nature, thus lowering

Christ's nature to the level of our own sinful condition. In a different way, the pantheistic theory of extreme sanctification accomplishes the same purpose by teaching that we fallen creatures can attain to Christ's holy condition. Here, we again see the consequences of pantheism—lowering the Creator while elevating the creature.

This extreme view of sanctification theorizes that a final generation of 144,000 living saints will become so spiritually developed, through the power of the Holy Spirit, that they will actually reach the same state of sinless perfection that Jesus had while in humanity. According to this idea, it is this perfect character that will enable the 144,000 to stand without Christ's mediation during the time of Jacob's trouble after the close of human probation. Those who hold this view acknowledge the need of Christ's grace for sins that are past but believe that it is possible to obtain absolute perfection in this life through sanctification. Thus, the basis of their hope, after probation, is the victory the Holy Spirit has given them over sin—not the atoning sacrifice of Jesus.

True victory . . . in Jesus

The Old Testament sanctuary service was God's object lesson to Israel to show how the substitutionary plan of salvation works. The centerpiece of that service was the sacrificial lamb. A lamb's blood had to be shed in order for sins to be forgiven. This was to teach that "without shedding of blood is no remission [of sin]" (Hebrews 9:22). God told the people through Moses, "It is the blood that maketh an atonement for the soul" (Leviticus 17:11). Faith in the shed blood of the sacrificial lamb, as a substitute for their sinful lives, was the Israelites's one and only hope of ever finding reconciliation with God.

The sacrificial lamb represented the Messiah who would one day come to redeem Israel. However, the nation of Israel in Jesus' day failed to make this connection, although prophet after prophet had clearly laid it out. Satan subtly led the Jewish leaders to the point that their hope of ultimate victory rested on the ousting of their visible oppressors—the Romans—rather than on the Messiah's substitutionary blood atonement.

But the New Testament writers picked up on this most vital connection and made it prominent in their teachings. It was the secret behind the power that attended their labors. The apostle Peter taught, "Forasmuch as ye know that ye were not redeemed with corruptible things, as silver and gold, . . . but with the precious blood of Christ, as of a lamb without blemish and without spot" (1 Peter 1:18, 19).

Other early church leaders taught that Christ had "purchased" the church "with his own blood" (Acts 20:28). They presented the blood of Jesus as the means by which we are to be "justified" and "saved from wrath" (Romans 5:9). From Paul, the Ephesians learned that in Christ "we have redemption through his blood," even "the forgiveness of sins" (Ephesians 1:7). The Gentiles also received the good news that though they were "strangers from the covenant of promise, having no hope, and without God in the world, now in Christ Jesus" they "are made nigh [to God] by the blood of Christ" (Ephesians 2:13). It is only through "the blood of his cross" that we can have peace with God (Colossians 1:20). It is the power of His blood that has gone before us into the sanctuary above and that allows us by faith to boldly access the throne room of God (see Hebrews 9:12; 10:19). It is through the blood of Jesus that we receive sanctification (see Hebrews 13:12). With His blood our sins are covered (see 1 John 1:9). That blood washes our robes, our characters, and makes them white (Revelation 1:5; 7:14). And, it is by "the blood of the Lamb" that we are able to overcome the devil and his accusations which stand against us in the judgement (Revelation 12:10, 11).

Yes, it is the substitutionary merits of the blood of Christ in which we are to place our total reliance for salvation. This has always been the truth and ever will be the truth.

Subtle subterfuge

The devil hates this theology of Christ's substitutionary blood atonement, because he knows it is the very gateway to heaven, the ladder of Jacob's dream. That is why he has sought to implant within Christianity "another gospel" (see Galatians 1:6). Satan's subtle subterfuge sounds very spiritual and logical, but in actuality it denies our total dependence on the substitutionary life and death of Christ.

What Satan is trying to do is to confuse us regarding the roles of the Godhead in the plan of salvation. *The result is a theology that substitutes the work of the Holy Spirit in the believer's life for the work that Jesus did in His behalf on the cross.* Such a teaching appears deeply spiritual because it appears to give God the redeeming credit in the person of the Holy Spirit. But in actuality, it takes our primary focus off what Jesus did for us at Calvary by placing too much emphasis on what the Holy Spirit is doing in us through sanctification. Though such a teaching seems to be glorifying God, it ultimately places the spotlight upon the creature and what is taking place within him or her. Christianity is prone to this deception because we Christians desire so earnestly to be liberated from our oppressor— our sinful nature—just as the Jews longed to be free from their oppressors, the Romans. Because of this, we have a tendency to shift our focus from what Christ did for us (which is something we can't see) and place it on the visible results of the Holy Spirit's work in our lives.

But the Holy Spirit is not our Savior; Jesus is. For one to become our substitute and surety required the shedding of blood. The Holy Spirit has never shed one drop of blood, because the Holy Spirit never became human (see Luke 24:39). It was Jesus who took humanity upon Himself so that "He would be enabled to pour out His blood in behalf of the fallen race" (*Manuscript Releases*, 17:26). It is the blood He shed as a human that qualifies the second member of the Godhead to be our Redeemer.

The Holy Spirit's role is not to draw attention to Himself nor to His powerful working in our lives. This is why He is represented by the invisible wind (see John 3:8). The intended work of the Holy Spirit is to convict us of our sinful state, to magnify the work Christ did in our behalf, and then to prepare us to meet the judgment by leading us to accept Jesus as our righteous Substitute (see John 16:8). Jesus said, "When he, the Spirit of truth, is come, he will guide you into all truth: for *he shall not speak of himself; . . . he shall glorify me*" (John 16: 13, 14, emphasis supplied).

But the serpent is still more subtle than any beast of the field. If we are not careful, he will beguile us to eat of his appealing theology, and we will think that we are getting hold of truth. We must try every spirit to see if what it is teaching is from God (see 1 John 4:1). One thing is certain: Every spirit that teaches that our only hope for salvation is found through faith in what Christ did as our substitute while in human flesh, is of God. If anyone teaches us to rely for salvation on anything else, he or she is teaching contrary to what Christ accomplished for us in human flesh. By this means we can know that such a teaching exhibits the spirit of antichrist (see 1 John 4:2, 3).

It is interesting to note that the Greek prefix *anti* in *antichrist* does not mean "against" Christ, as it might seem on the surface. The meaning here is "in place of" or "a substitute for." While the true gospel makes the Creator a substitute for the creature, Satan's version seeks to substitute the creature into the roll of the Creator. Whereas God created man in His image, man seeks to create a god that is in his image. Amazingly, the pope has consistently claimed in his encyclicals that he is the "Vicar of Christ," which means "Substitute for Christ," and it's inscribed right in the pope's tiara or official ceremonial crown. Here, again, we have the fundamental principle in the great controversy played out in the issue about how and by whom God saves us. There is but one being capable of being a substitute, and consequently a mediator, between God and man—the God/man, Jesus Christ (see 1 Timothy 2:5). In light of this truth, how vital it is that the church make Jesus her focal point of thought and teaching if she ever hopes to unite with the Spirit in giving the world an invitation to enter the eternal rest to be found in Jesus' substitutionary saving work (see Revelation 22:17).

Among Adventists there has always been a lot of discussion concerning victory over sin. And many have made the fatal mistake of thinking that we must gain the victory over sin before we can have assurance of our acceptance with God. But Abraham, being a true example of saving faith, was justified unto eternal life and made righteous in God's eyes before he was ever circumcised (see Romans 4:1-13). Spiritual circumcision is defined as "putting off the body of the sins of the flesh" (Colossians 2:11). It is the painful process of having embedded sins cut out of the life through the process of sanctification.

But please note, just as Abraham was considered righteous *before* he underwent physical circumcision, so we are delared righteous by God *before* we undergo spiritual circumcision. The one who believes the gospel of Christ receives righteousness at the beginning of his religious experience, not as a result of his religious experience. That's why we are told,

> If you see your sinfulness, do not wait to make yourself better. How many there are who think they are not good enough to come to Christ. . . Jesus loves to have us come to Him just as we are, sinful, helpless, dependent. We may come with all our weakness, our folly, our sinfulness, and fall at His feet in penitence. . . Do not wait to feel that you are made whole, but say, "I believe it ; it is so, not because I feel it, but because God has promised" (*Manuscript Releases*, vol. 17, 31, 51, 52).

As the old hymn says, "If we tarry till we're better, we will never come at all."

Overcoming sin in the life is not what gains us acceptance with God. Our only acceptance is found in and through Christ's obedience in our behalf (see Isaiah 26:12; Hebrews 4:3). If we focus on attaining certain standards held up for us in inspired writings, without looking to Christ, then our ship is sunk before we even set sail. Looking to Christ means we trust His substitutionary merits as the only means by which we can be made acceptable to God. This will be our experience only as we discern the fact that we will always fall short in trying to reach the standard. The divine requirements of holiness are held up before us in order to teach us that it is utterly impossible for us to meet them by any power within ourselves. As the condition of eternal life, God requires a level of obedience that is absolutely impossible for us to attain.

Why? Why would God do this?

First, as the realization begins to sink into our minds that we cannot, through our human obedience, attain to the standard that the law requires, it cures us of "navel gazing." This is to say, we will cease to look within ourselves for any hope of, or signs of, righteousness. It also means that we will see the folly of peering into the merits of anyone else to find holiness. It will cause us to search outside of corrupted humanity for a substitute source of righteousness that will enable us to meet the stated requirements. And that source can only be found in Christ! "No man can look within himself and find anything in his character that will recommend him to God, or make his acceptance sure. . . Jesus alone is our Redeemer, our Advocate and Mediator; in Him is our only hope for pardon, peace, and righteousness" (*Selected Messages*, 1:332, 333).

The law reveals where we fall short, thus serving as a "schoolmaster to bring us to Christ, that we might be justified" (Galatians 3:24). Ellen White lays out this process in a most beautiful way in these words:

The less we see to esteem in ourselves, the more we shall see to esteem in the infinite purity and loveliness of our Saviour. A view of our sinfulness drives us to Him who can pardon; and when the soul, realizing its helplesness, reaches out after Christ, He will reveal Himself in power. The more our sense of need drives us to Him and to the word of God, the more exalted views we shall have of His character, and the more fully we shall reflect His image (*Steps to Christ*, 65).

The law leads us to trust, not in our own character development, but rather in the character that Christ developed in humanity. He is my saving Substitute. "Christ's character stands in place of your character, and you are accepted before God just as if you had not sinned" (*Steps to Christ*, 62). Even though a process of reformation begins in our own human character, Christ's substitutionary character will forever remain as the basis of our righteousness and salvation. The everlasting gospel declares that His saving, substitutionary merits are not temporary but eternal. For the creature, "the efforts for perfection of Christian character will continue for eternity" (*Testimonies for the Church,* 4:520).

So victory over sin is possible only by trusting in Christ's atoning blood and claiming His obedience as having already met the standard for us. As long as we trust, even "partly," to "the performance of certain duties [on our part] for acceptance with Him," we will have "no victories" (*Selected Messages*, 1:353).

Oh, how many conscientious souls there are among us who are sincerely trying to obey what they feel is God's ideal high calling! They carefully try to bring their lives into conformity with certain standards obviously called for by inspired counsels. To such I would say, "Don't ever lose your desire to honor God by doing 'those things that are pleasing in his sight' " (1 John 3:22). We must never forget that only those who "are putting forth humble efforts to live up to the requirements of God" does He regard "as obedient children, and the righteousness of Christ is imputed unto them" (*Our High Calling*, 51). If we remain satisfied with our rotten, sinful characters, having no real burden to be changed, then we will surely fail in becoming like Christ. Such will be disappointed at His coming to realize that He will not perform a miracle to change them then (see *Adventist Home*, 16). Such will be left to face the final judgement on the merits of their own characters instead of the merits of Christ's substitutionary perfection.

We need to recognize the need to put forth efforts to live up to all that God has asked of His people. But I would also urge us all to understand that God is reasonable in what He demands of us in our fallen condition. He remembers that we are but human; He wants us to come to a settled understanding that *His* ability to meet the law's demands and *our* ability to do so are quite different. He is the only one who can perfectly meet the demands of His own law. The Lord wants us to learn, as Uzzah did, that if human hands try to touch the law, through dependence to any degree on our own obedience to it, it simply will not work! And the result will be disastrous for ourselves. As the earthly sanctuary services taught, only the High Priest can approach the ark that contains the law without being destroyed! "Since we are sinful, unholy, we cannot perfectly obey the holy law" (*Steps to Christ*, 62).

God seeks to teach us this same lesson through the two covenants (see *Patriarchs and Prophets*, 370-373). The first, or old covenant, is the one He gave to Israel at Sinai. He asked them to keep his commandments. This the Israelites tried to do in their own strength, but understandably failed. Then, after showing them the futility of trying on their own to keep His requirements, God proposed to them a second covenant. This is also called the "new" covenant and the "everlasting" covenant.

It required only that the people admit that they simply were not able to perfectly obey God's holy law and that they have faith that He would perform the keeping of His law in their behalf. To illustrate this lesson, God told them, "Go, kill a lamb. Its unblemished condition and spilled blood will represent your Savior, and I will count its death as though you yourself have perfectly obeyed the law."

This was actually the same covenant that He had previously made with their father Abraham, which is why it is also referred to as the "Abrahamic covenant." This "new covenant" is eternally effective because Jesus *is the Lamb slain* and "the mediator" of it (Hebrews 8:6; 12:24).

Likewise, God is trying to teach us the same principle He taught ancient Israel. He allows us to attempt the impossibility of meeting the law's requirements in order to show us our limited capacity both to do and to be what He says we should be. Then, as we realize that the required standard of obedience is beyond us, He impresses us with a deeper revelation that Jesus' life and death met the law's demands in our behalf. Even more, through our faith in that sacrifice, He counts it as though *we* did it! "The glory of the gospel of grace through the imputed righteousness of Christ, provides no other way of salvation than through obedience to the law of God in the person of Jesus Christ, the divine Substitute. . . The only means of salvation is provided under the Abrahamic covenant" (*Signs of the Times*, 5 September 1892). "Before this faith came, we were held prisoners by the law, locked up until faith should be revealed" (Galatians 3:23, NIV).

Jesus only

God has tried to use many methods to teach us the difference between ourselves (the creature) and Himself (the Creator). Remember the time Peter, James, and John took a trip with Jesus to the top of the Mount of Transfiguration? While they were there with Jesus, He suddenly was transformed into the appearance He will have at the Second Coming.

As the disciples tried to look at Him through the glory of His presence, they heard Moses and Elijah talking with Him. Then Peter, not clearly distinguishing between Christ and the creatures surrounding Him, suggested that they build three places of worship there on the mountain—one for Jesus, one for Moses, and one for Elijah. But before he could even get his proposal all out, God spoke to them, "This is my beloved Son, in whom I am well pleased; hear ye him" (Matthew 17:5).

When they heard that voice, the disciples dropped to the ground in fear. As they hid their faces in the dirt, afraid for their very lives, Jesus walked over and "touched them, and said, Arise, and be not afraid. And when they had lifted up their eyes, they saw no man, save Jesus only" (verses 7, 8).

This brings us to another reason why God's law asks of us that which it is not possible for us to perform in our sinful natures. It wasn't set up this way for arbitrary reasons. It has to do with the difference in God's capacity as Creator compared to our capacity as His creatures. It's the difference in ability between the Infinite and the finite. Herein lies the main truth that will result in God's ultimate victory in the great controversy.

Because they have not recognized this distinction sufficiently, many Seventh-day Adventists honestly believe in the "final generation" theory. This theory teaches that a final generation of 144,000 saints will become so spiritually developed through the Holy Spirit's work in their lives (sanctification) that they will no longer require the mediation of Christ after probation closes. Those who defend this idea feel that to challenge it is to threaten sacred truth. They see those who believe we will still need mediation after the close of human probation as denying God's power and what it can accomplish in our lives. Like Lucifer, they maintain, "I will be like the most High" (Isaiah 14:14).

But what really establishes God's power is when the Holy Spirit finally pierces all our preconceived, pantheistic ideas and enlightens our minds with the glory of God. He does this by clearly distinguishing just who we are in relationship to who He is; what His role, as God, is in contrast to what our role is as His creatures. And this He has promised to do. "These things hast thou done, and I kept silence; thou thoughtest that I was altogether such an one as thyself: but I will reprove thee, and set them [our deficiencies] in order before thine eyes" (Psalm 50:21).

When this lesson is brought home to us, we will experience what Job experienced when he finally realized God's holy nature in contrast to his own humanity. Job said, "I have heard of thee by the hearing of the ear: but now mine eye seeth thee [how holy God is]. Wherefore I abhor myself, and repent in dust and ashes" (Job 42:5, 6). We will feel as did Peter when he said, "Depart from me; for I am a sinful man, O Lord" (Luke 5:8).

Do you see? God is trying to solve the original sin problem, a problem that began with the creature's "ambition to be equal with God" (*Testimonies for the Church*, 5:702). God accomplishes this by dissolving the creature's secret ambition to play God, along with his delusion that he can match the Lord's state of holiness. This concern strikes at the very root of the entire great-controversy issue, from beginning to end. "He [Satan] desired to enter into the divine counsels and purposes, from which he was excluded by his own inability, as a created being, to comprehend the wisdom of the Infinite One. It was this ambitious pride that led to his rebellion, and *by the same means he seeks to cause the ruin of man*" (Ibid., emphasis supplied).

Calvary dismantles this "original sin" syndrome, that leads the creature to think he can become like God and stand on his own merits. It does this by showing the creature that without God he "can do nothing" (John 15:5). God's primary purpose in the plan of restoration is not to demonstrate what we creatures can do but to show the distinction between His capabilities and ours. The plan of salvation enables us fallen creatures to re-adjust our center of focus off ourselves and on to Him. And it is through this process that we are actually sanctified. Sanctifica-tion, the work going on inside of us, occurs only as we focus on justification, the work accomplished outside of us by Jesus Christ.

God's people desperately need to understand this point. Unless we do, we are going to go into the final conflict clothed, not with the righteousness of Jesus Christ, but cloaked with the garments of carnal pride and self-sufficiency. We are going to be like the man who showed up at the wedding feast without the required wedding garment (see Matthew 22:1-14). In Bible sym-bolism, a garment represents character. No doubt the man felt the garment (character) he had on was good enough. And no doubt many of us have been led to believe that we will be fit to go into the Lamb's marriage supper by virtue of what has taken place in our characters through our own cooperation with the Holy Spirit during the sanctification process.

We must be learning now to implicitly trust in Jesus to the very end, as our "righteousness, and sanctification, and redemp-tion" (1 Corinthians 1:30).

> He [mankind] may deceive himself in regard to this matter. . . . Christ's righteousness alone can avail for his salvation, and this is the gift of God. This is the wedding garment in which you may appear as a welcome guest at the marriage supper of the Lamb (*Selected Messages*, 1:331).

What it all boils down to is an issue of pride on the part of the creature. The carnal person likes to think he has it all to-gether when it comes to spiritual things. He is desperately try-ing to be satisfied with his own condition of Christian character. He tells himself, "I am rich, and increased with goods, and have need of nothing" (Revelation 3:17). It is a pleasant thought to him that though others may be falling short of the standard he can overcome anything that confronts him. That's why he gauges his holiness by how well he matches up to other sinners. He is on a mad march to perfect a character that will be good enough to save himself. He tenaciously holds on to spiritual doctrines that are compatible with his deceived state. But the carnal person desperately needs to be humbled for his own eternal benefit. And that is what Calvary is for. When he finally consents to look upon, and measure himself, by the One who hangs upon the cross, the old man of sin dies, and he becomes a new creature in Christ Jesus.

But until the carnal person humbles himself in penitence and humiliation before God at Calvary, he is both in danger and dangerous. He is most dangerous when he tries to become religious without first becoming converted. He trusts in his ability to keep from committing outward acts of sin. To him, this is an indication of his spiritual advancement and the focal point of his religion. Paul identifies such religion as "will worship" (see Colossians 2:21-23). Because he has not the power stemming from a love-response relationship with Christ—the power that leads to genuine obedience—he begins to invent ways to obey what he thinks are God's requirements.

> The effort to earn salvation by one's own works inevitably leads men to pile up human exactions as a barrier against sin. For, seeing that they fail to keep the law, they will devise rules and regulations of their own to force themselves to obey. All this turns the mind away from God to self (*Thoughts From the Mount of Blessing*, 123).

As we start forcing ourselves to obey when, deep down, we are doing it from a wrong motive, this is the germination of the process that forms the beast power. It makes us angry with God and intolerant of others. It brews within our souls another batch of that "wine of the wrath of her [Babylon's] fornication" (Revelation 18:3). And, interestingly enough, that wine begins to ferment as we trample underfoot the golden rule and disregard the religious liberty of others by forcing upon them the criteria of obedience we have set up for ourselves.

A system of human invention, with its multitudinous exactions, will lead its advocates to judge all who come short of the prescribed human standard. The atmosphere of selfish and narrow criticism stifles the noble and generous emotions, and causes men to become self-centered judges and petty spies. The Pharisees were of this class. They came forth from their religious services, not humbled with a sense of their own weakness. . . . They came forth filled with spiritual pride (*Thoughts From the Mount of Blessing*, 122, 123).

We have been warned that "he who looses sight of his entire dependence upon God is sure to fall" (*Gospel Workers*, 322). But justification by faith leads us away from this self-dependency and centers our entire hopes upon the Savior. This is why Ellen White, when asked to define justification by faith, replied, "It is the work of God in laying the glory of man in the dust, and doing for man that which it is not in his power (character) to do for himself" (*The Faith I Live By*, 111).

May God help us to discern clearly just how much we need Jesus!

My hope is built on nothing less, Than Jesus' blood and righteousness;
I dare not trust the sweetest frame, But wholly lean on Jesus' name.

SAVING BLOOD

When darkness seems to veil His face, I rest on His unchanging
grace;
In every high and stormy gale, My anchor holds within the veil.

His oath, His covenant, and blood, Support me in the whelming
flood;
When all around my soul gives way, He then is all my hope and
stay.

When He shall come with trumpet sound, O may I then in Him be
found;
Clad in His righteousness alone, Faultless to stand before His
throne.

On Christ, the solid Rock, I stand; All other ground is sinking
sand,
All other ground is sinking sand.

Edward Mote

CHAPTER
15

Who Shall Be Able To Stand?

One of the greatest questions in the entire Bible is the one posed by the Old Testament prophet Malachi. Referring to Christ's second coming, Malachi asks, "But who may abide the day of his coming? and who shall stand when he appeareth?" (Malachi 3:2). This question is of vital importance to everyone who looks for Christ's soon return. We must know, from the Bible, how to prepare ourselves and others for this great event.

In the last chapter, we began to examine the teaching that God's people must be spiritually able to stand without Christ's mediation after the close of probation. Those who accept this idea often believe that in order to stand during this awful time we will have to have a character that equals the character of Christ during His time on earth. This concept has led to the idea that a final generation of 144,000 living saints will vindicate God's character to the universe through what the Holy Spirit has accomplished in them.

In evaluating such an idea, it is vital that we understand the difference between justification (what Christ did on the cross in our behalf) and sanctification (what the Holy Spirit does daily in us). Only by means of justification will any of us be saved. "As the penitent sinner, contrite before God, discerns Christ's atonement in his behalf, and accepts this atonement as his only hope in this life and the future life, his sins are pardoned. This is justification by faith" (*Manuscript Releases*, 9:301). Here we see that our spiritual standing throughout eternity will be undergirded by justification. In eternity, our legal right to life will never be based on what we are, or even what we will become through the ceaseless ages. Instead, our life will always be wrapped up in our faith in what Christ did for us, the justification of our souls.

This in no way negates the importance of sanctification. It simply places sanctification in a right relationship to the work that God does in justification. Sanctification of the soul is not, and never will be, the salvation of the soul. People are saved through justification. That's why Ellen White could state that once we are in a justified state, "holiness [the standard of the law] finds that it has nothing more to require" (*Christ's Object Lessons*, 162).

Sanctification is merely the outward demonstration of our willingness to cooperate with God. It shows that we have undergone an attitude change about bringing our lives into obedience to His will. Such a change is made evident by our feeble efforts to keep His law.

But we must never confuse what God does in us with what He did for us on the cross. If we do, we will inevitably end up with the Roman Catholic version of justification by faith, a position that Luther spent all his energies combatting. That subtle doctrine teaches that by cooperation with God, through obedience, we increase our status of justification and literally become righteous in this life. The Reformation principle, on the other hand, held that righteousness can be realized only by accepting Christ's grace through faith—from start to finish, from the cross to the crown! To men like Luther and Calvin, to be decleared just by Christ's intercessory merits was the pinnacle of the Christian's experience. To put it another way, a repentant position at the foot of the cross is the highest place which we can attain.

The unfallen universe fully realizes this fact. Yet some of us blindly continue to tell ourselves that someday, while in a fallen condition and while still on this planet, we are going to demonstrate the same perfect obedience that Jesus demonstrated! We also pride ourselves with the exaggerated thought that when we do so, we are somehow going to convince the universe that God is really innocent of Satan's original charge that His law is too arbitrary and strict!

Although the beauty of the law's precepts will be demonstrated in our lives through the Lord's enabling grace, He is not ultimately dependent on this for His vindication. Reality is that God has *already* vindicated Himself before the universe. He answered Satan's charges when He came as the second Adam and lived a life of obedience. It is Christ that "would fully vindicate His Father's law" (*Review and Herald*, 3 March 1874). When He died, Satan fell "as lightning . . . from heaven" (Luke 10:18).

The idea that we can reach a state of inherent righteousness through sanctification and thus vindicate God's character may allow us to establish some sense of self-worth through our obedient behavior, but sooner or later we must face the fact that we can find self-worth only in Jesus. He must increase, and we must decrease. In terms of our sanctification, God is not measuring performance but commitment. What matters to Him is the direction we are moving, not perfect performance. To say it another way, if we are growing in grace, then we are going to heaven because of justification.

It is not what we are that will get us through the time of trouble but who we know. "If you would stand through the time of trouble, *you must know Christ,* and appropriate the gift of his righteousness, which he imputes [that's justification] to the repentant sinner" (*Review and Herald,* 22 November 1892). To know Christ means to know Him as the One who saves through His substitutionary merits.

Notice this amazing verse in Hebrews. "For by one offering he hath perfected for ever them that are sanctified" (10:14). Within Adventist circles, this verse has often been interpreted to mean that at some future time God will make perfect those who become fully sanctified. But this is not what the scripture is saying. Right up front, it tells us that "by one offering," meaning by what Christ did at Calvary, He considers all who are in the sanctification process as being perfect forever! He says to us, "Listen! Because of My infinite sacrifice, I'll account you as perfect throughout the ceaseless ages of eternity if you will agree to let Me begin working on you now."

It really is a "pie in the sky" idea to believe that we will ever match Christ's record, in this life or even in the future life. Exodus 15:11 is a Scripture text for all time: "Who is like unto thee, O Lord, among the gods? who is like thee, glorious in holiness, fearful in praises, doing wonders?" And Ellen White adds,

> He [Jesus] is a perfect and holy example, given for us to imitate. We cannot equal the pattern; but we shall not be approved of God if we do not copy it and, according to the ability which God has given, resemble it (*Testimonies for the Church*, 2:549).

> He had a mighty influence, for He was the Son of God. We are so far beneath Him and so far deficient, that, do the very best we can, our efforts will be poor. . . . But why should we not educate ourselves to come just as near to the pattern as it is possible for us to do, that we may have the greatest possible influence upon the people? (Ibid., 617, 618).

Here is the real reason we should be striving to bring our lives into conformity to the testimony of Jesus. The closer we can come to following the Lord's counsel, as has been revealed through His prophets, the more influence we will possess to draw others to Jesus.

Without a mediator?

The hardest lesson for fallen humanity to learn is this: As long as we are confined to this carnal nature, even our acts of obedience are tainted with sin! This means that *all* the things we do right ascend to the heavenly sanctuary in a defiled state and require the application of Christ's atoning blood to make them pure and acceptable to God.

Regarding the righteous actions of "true believers," Ellen White tells us that these good deeds are brought about by the work of the Holy Spirit in their lives. Then she adds,

> . . . but passing through the corrupt channels of humanity, they are so defiled that unless purified by blood, they can never be of value with God. They ascend (to the heavenly sanctuary) not in spotless purity, and unless the Intercessor, who is at God's right hand, presents and purifies all by His righteousness, it is not acceptable to God. . . . Oh, that all may see that everything in obedience, in penitence, in praise and thanksgiving, must be placed upon the glowing fire of the righteousness of Christ (*Selected Messages*, 1:344, 345).

Consider it this way. Suppose I offered you a drink of pure, clean, distilled water. Would you have any hesitency about drinking it? Of course not. But what if I went out and found an old dirty, plastic jug in a ditch along the highway, poured the clean water into it, and then offered you a drink? You see, the work that the Holy Spirit does in us is pure and clean. But the problem lies in the filthy containers in which He performs the work. The carnal natures we possess, even after we are converted, are like that dirty plastic jug. But what if I then took the water, which had become contaminated by being in the jug, and ran it through a distiller and then through a water filter. Would it now be fit to drink once again? Yes! Praise God for the distilling, purifying effects of Christ's merits in our behalf in the sanctuary above!

Such an understanding of how faith and works operate in the salvation process should humble our haughty, carnal attitudes concerning what we accomplish in this life. It should prevent us from thinking we can do something that will be more acceptable in God's sight than what someone else can do. "There is none righteous, no, not one" (Romans 3:10). We are like the lepers in Christ's day. As God draws near, we must yell out "Unclean! Unclean!" Like Isaiah, when he went into the temple of God and came face to face with true righteousness (see Isaiah 6:5), we must recognize our undone condition.

Failure to comprehend this truth is the real root of Laodicea's failure to sense her need of God. This is why Martin Luther declared:

> Every good work of the saints while pilgrims in this world is sin. I have taught that our good works are of such a kind as cannot bear the judgment of God. . . . I repeat, that a good work in itself is unclean if the covering cloud of grace is removed (*Early Theological Works*, XVI:318-354).

Inspiration supports Luther's conclusion. The wise man said, "For there is not a just man upon earth, that doeth good, and sinneth not" (Ecclesiastes 7:20). Ellen White taught that "man's obedience can be made perfect only by the incense of Christ's righteousness, which fills with divine fragrance every act of obedience" (*The Acts of the Apostles*, 532). No doubt this is the same lesson Isaiah was trying to teach when he wrote, "But we are all as an unclean thing, and all our righteousnesses are as filthy rags" (Isaiah 64:6). And this is the way it is going to be all the way down to the Second Coming.

But what about those statements in which Ellen White said we "are to stand in the sight of a holy God without a mediator" (*The Great Controversy*, 425)? And what about other related statements concerning the events surrounding the close of probation? (See *Early Writings*, 48, 71, 280, 281.)

Those who take an extreme view of sanctification wrest these statements to mean that because of the Holy Spirit's work in us we will not require Christ's intercessory merits after the close of probation. Of course, none of God's people will be living lives of wilful sin during this time. By this time they will have come to respect God so much that they would rather die than knowingly transgress His law. But they will still be confined to a human nature that pollutes even their good works with sinfulness. This fact continues to make them dependent upon Christ's atoning grace even after probation is closed. The close of probation is the time when the "grace store" closes, and no more oil can be purchased by foolish virgins. And what does that oil represent? "That oil is the righteousness of Christ" (*Testimonies to Ministers*, 234). After probation closes, no one will be able to trade his carnal rags for Christ's riches.

When Michael stands up from His mediation and probation closes, the judgment is completed, and the eternal destiny of every soul is fixed forever. He will irrevocably pronounce as eternally righteous ("righteous still" or "righteous from henceforth") all who have trusted in His righteousness and who have hidden themselves under the shelter of His grace. At the same time, He will pronounce those who have chosen not to get under His shelter of grace as forever filthy ("filthy still" or "filthy from henceforth"; see Revelation 22:11). This is why Ellen White lamented the cases of the unrighteous by saying, "Oh, how many I saw in the time of trouble without a shelter" (*Early Writings*, 71). "Unsheltered by divine grace, they have no protection from the wicked one. . ." she wrote in another place. "In that day, multitudes will desire the shelter of God's mercy which they have so long despised" (*The Great Controversy*, 629).

Ellen White was trying to make the point that Christ's active role as Mediator will one day cease. If we haven't gone to Christ for justification by the time His work ceases in the sanctuary we will have no hope of ever receiving it after He leaves.

But if we are under the benefits of His saving blood before probation closes, that same mediating grace will carry us through the time of trouble. Christ's covering grace is what fits us to stand in the presence of a holy God at the Second Coming. Abiding under the shelter of Christ's grace is the only answer that can satisfy Malachi's question, "Who may abide the day of his coming? and who shall stand when he appeareth?" (Malachi 3:2). As King David declared, "For in the time of trouble he shall hide me in his pavilion" (Psalm 27:5).

This is what Ellen White saw when in vision she witnessed the Second Advent of our Lord. The question was asked, " 'Who shall be able to stand?' " Jesus replied, " 'Those who have clean hands and pure hearts shall be able to stand.' " That's where many stop reading. But let's allow Him to finish His sentence: " 'My grace is sufficient for you' " (see *Testimonies for the Church*, 1:60; Psalm 24:3-5).

It is just as the book of Hebrews says: "Wherefore he [Jesus Christ] is able also to save them to the uttermost that come unto God by him, seeing he ever liveth to make intercession for them" (Hebrews 7:25). This is why it is called the *everlasting* gospel. Sustaining grace was in place before sin ever entered the picture, and it will play a sustaining role in the universe even after sin has been destroyed. Even today, it is Christ's mediatorial grace that keeps intact even worlds that have never fallen (see *Messages to Young People*, 254). A hundred trillion years down eternity's corridor, the fact that we are under the eternal umbrella of Christ's meritorious grace will be the only legal right any of us will have to be in God's kingdom. The everlasting gospel is designed to show us just how eternally dependent we are upon Jesus. Once again, it is the antidote to the Great Controversy syndrome. Any teaching that does not serve this purpose is out of harmony with the message of the first angel (see Revelation 14:6).

The interpretation that we must reach a perfect level of holiness through the Holy Spirit's sanctifying power or else be unable to endure the time of trouble is straining the meaning of certain inspired statements. It places before us an ideal that is impossible to achieve and that will ultimately either unsettle our faith in the plan of salvation or seal our fate in bogus creature worship. It breeds rebellion and hatred towards God because it portrays Him as a hard taskmaster, a stern judge who requires the impossible.

Failure to live up to such unrealistic ideas is why many have concluded that God is unreasonable and consequently have left the faith. No wonder we lose so many who join us. We draw them into the church with the precious message of Christ's covering righteousness and then turn right around and tell them they must eventually develop a state of righteousness comparable to that which Jesus had—or be lost during the time of trouble! Paul's stinging reproof to the Galatians no doubt applies to us today, "O foolish Galatians, who hath bewitched you? . . . Are ye so foolish? having begun in the Spirit [through justification], are ye now made perfect by the flesh [by what you do in this life]?" (Galatians 3:1, 3).

For a long time now, God has been trying to help us steer clear of this satanic delusion. In fact, this was the intended result of the message given in 1888. Speaking of the experience of some who understood righteousness by faith, A. T. Jones wrote,

> We were glad of the news that God had righteousness that would pass the judgment and would stand accepted in His sight. A righteousness that is a good deal better than anything that people could manufacture by years and years of hard work. People had worn out their souls almost, trying to manufacture a sufficient degree of righteousness to stand through the time of trouble, and meet the Saviour in peace when He comes, but they had not accomplished it. These were so glad to find out that God had already manufactured a robe of righteousness and offered it as a free gift to everyone who would take it, that it would answer now, and in the time of the plagues, and in the time of the judgment, and to all eternity. . . . You know the time was when we actually sat

down and cried because we could not do well enough to satisfy our own estimate of right doing; and as we were expecting the Lord to come soon, we dreaded the news that it was so near; for how in the world were we going to be ready? (*General Conference Bulletin*, 1893).

Historically, Adventism has created a parched theological landscape with its focus on perfection through obedience. But this will create a generation that is ready for "the times of refreshing," the outpouring of the "latter rain," which is the message of a perfection based solely on the merits of Christ's achievements.

For the most part, mainstream Adventist theology has corrected false views that distort the pure gospel. However, some among us still are determined to hang on to this strained, "final-generation" theory. Many of these have become bitter and condemning of church leaders who have tried to help them correct these theological errors. In their blindness, they have denounced these leaders as "new theologians" and destroyers of the true Adventist faith. But this is only a smokescreen behind which these misguided souls hide their own personal frustrations. They have given it—the attempt to reach a state of sinlessness—their best try, and if they were honest would admit that it just doesn't work. Like the Pharisees of old, their pride keeps them from admitting their failure, and they denounce as error the very truth that would correct their extreme views.

Why do we have such a difficult time settling into the truth that "while sin is forgiven in this life, its results [the carnal nature] are not now wholly removed. *It is at His coming* that Christ is to 'change our vile body, that it may be fashioned like unto his glorious body' (Phil.3:21)" (*Selected Messages*, 2:33, emphasis supplied). "We cannot say, 'I am sinless,' till this vile body is changed and fashioned like unto His glorious body" (*Signs of the Times*, 23 March 1888). Such a realization will all the more help us become riveted on the great hope of Christ's soon return, because that is when we will be completely liberated from our carnal natures that are antagonistic to our spiritual desires.

Building another ark

The fact that we will still require Christ's grace to cover us even after probation closes is illustrated by the world's destruction at the time of the Flood. The open door to the ark represented God's offer to help people through the terrible events ahead. As long as that door of probation was open, anyone could get on the boat. But the very second that door closed, the time of opportunity had passed. People were either on the boat or they were not. And those who were not on board had absolutely no hope of ever getting on, regardless of how badly they wanted to. So it will be with those living through the last days up to the very time when Jesus steps out of the sanctuary.

But what about those that were inside the ark? Now that probation had closed, were they dependent on the work they had done in building the ship to carry them safely through the terrible storm? Or were they still dependent on God to help them through the Flood? Did the ark make it safely through that indescribable catastrophe because God had specified its design and because Noah had followed those instructions precisely? Or was there an intervening hand involved?

After Noah had done all in his power to make every part of the work correct, it was impossible that it could of itself withstand the violence of the storm. . . All that men could do was done to make the work perfect; yet after all, God alone could preserve the building upon the angry, heaving billows, by His miraculous power (*Spiritual Gifts*, 3:66).

It was Christ who kept the ark safe amid the roaring, seething billows, because its inmates had faith in

169

His power to preserve them (*SDA Bible Commentary*, 1:1091; see also *Early Writings*, 284).

It will be the same for the saints during the catastrophic events of the end time. And during that time, we will need the same kind of faith that Noah and his family exhibited in order to get safely through the time of trouble before Jesus comes. God's people will not be trusting to a finished job of character building, no matter how perfectly the job may have been carried out by obeying divine counsel. Instead, they will go through the time of trouble by faith in the perpetual, interceding merits of their crucified and risen Savior.

The Lord is practical and reasonable in His requirements. He is not asking us to reach a sinless state before we can feel at ease with our spiritual growth. It's true that He asks us to put everything we possibly can into the development of our spiritual characters, but He has promised to cover us with His grace each step of the way. He has told us to rest assured that He will never leave us or forsake us. We need not be stressed with worry about what we must be in the future. Instead, we need to focus only on living daily by trusting the promises of God.

Two of those promises provide us with an outline of how our final redemption will be accomplished. All that is required to activate these promises is a willingness to cooperate with the heavenly intelligences in their work. If we agree to do that, then we can with certainty believe Paul when he said, "I am confident of this: that the One who has begun His good work in you will go on developing it until the day of Jesus Christ" (Philipians 1:6, Phillips).

Just what form that finished work of sanctification will be, we do not know. The apostle John has told us, "Beloved, now are we the sons of God [justification], and it doth not yet appear what we shall be [sanctification and glorification]: but we know that, when he shall appear, we shall be like him; for we shall see him as he is" (1 John 3:2).

Who Shall Be Able To Stand?

The blood that Jesus once shed for me,
As my Redeemer upon the tree,
The blood that sets the prisoner free,
Will never lose its power.
It gives us access to God on high,
From "far off places" it brings us nigh,
To precious blessings that never die,
It will never lose its power.
It is a shelter for rich and poor,
It is to heaven the open door,
The sinner's merit evermore,
It will never lose its power.
And when with the blood-washed throng,
We sing in glory redemption's song,
We'll pass the glorious truth along,
It has never lost its power.
It will never lose its power,
It will never lose its power,
The blood that cleanses from all sin,
Will never lose its power.

Mrs. C. D. Martin

CHAPTER 16

The Obedience of Faith

In this book we have tended to focus more on God's love, grace, and mercy rather than His justice. This is because we are to make these merciful aspects of God's character the prominent features as we present Him to the church and the world. Our heavenly Father's love and grace and mercy are the most powerful tools to draw men and women into a commitment to a life of total devotion to Him.

This is how the Lord presented Himself to Moses on Mount Sinai. Moses had asked the Lord to preach him a sermon regarding His character. Before God brought Moses into His direct presence, He hid him in the shelter of a rock. And we, too, will need to be hidden under the "grace shelter" of Christ, the living Rock, before we can stand in God's direct presence at the Second Coming. Then,

the Lord passed by before him [Moses], and proclaimed, the Lord, the Lord God, merciful and gracious, longsuffering, and abundant in goodness and truth, keeping mercy for thousands, forgiving iniquity and transgression and sin, and that will by no means clear the guilty; visiting the iniquity of the fathers upon the children, and upon the children's children, unto the third and to the fourth generation (Exodus 34:6, 7).

Please notice that the Lord Himself gave prominence to His mercy and grace and listed these aspects of His character before His justice. But neither did He omit His justice.

We may with assurance hang our helpless souls upon Christ's grace, but we must never deny or seek to evade the fact that God's justice will forever remain intact. If we lose sight of God's justice, Paul's words will apply to us: "They profess that they know God; but in works they deny him" (Titus 1:16). The same perfect obedience and perfection of character that God required of Adam before the fall is still what He requires of us today. In focusing on God's love and grace and mercy, I am in no way suggesting that the law has been abolished or somehow altered to meet us in our sinful state. What I am trying to bring out is the fact that the only possible way for any of us to meet the just demands of God's law is through justification by faith in the merits of Jesus Christ as our substitute.

Jesus alone succeeded where Adam failed and fulfilled the law's demands for us. Now He offers that perfect obedience to each one of us. He accepts our best efforts, taking into consideration our individual spheres of ability and limiting circumstances. But our acceptance is based, not on our performance, but on Jesus' performance. "Jesus loves His children, even if they err. . . . He keeps His eye upon them, and when they do their best, calling upon God for His help, be assured the service will be accepted, although imperfect. . . . Jesus makes up for our unavoidable deficiencies" (*Selected Messages*, 3:195, 196). But please note, this beautiful truth concerning God's grace does not negate the fact that "God will not accept a willfully imperfect service" (*Review and Herald*, 3 September 1901).

This is the real beauty of the plan of salvation. God can remain just while justifying the sinner. He can fully exercise His grace and yet keep His justice intact. "God always demanded good works, the law demands it, but because man placed himself in sin where his good works were valueless, Jesus' righteousness alone can avail" (*SDA Bible Commentary*, 6:1071). Obedience rendered in our fallen state will never be good enough, because of the weakness of our human nature (see Romans 8:3). The only obedience that is of value to God is an obedience that relies totally on faith. "Probation would be granted him [fallen man] in which, through a life of repentance, and faith in the atonement of the Son of God, he might be redeemed from his transgression of the Father's law, and thus be elevated to a position where his efforts to keep that law could be accepted" (*Signs of the Times*, 30 January 1879).

Even though we recognize that our human efforts to keep the law of God will always fall short of the mark, this fact should not cause us to take a nonchalant attitude toward obedience. *Obedience is important. But it is an obedience that is not legalistic in nature but an obedience that relies totally on Christ's merits for its acceptance.* Ellen White speaks of an "obedience made possible by his [Christ's] merits" (*Review and Herald*, 29 April 1902). "By His [Jesus'] perfect obedience," she wrote, "He has made it possible for every human being to obey God's commandments" (*Christ's Object Lessons*, 312). However, if we conclude that we need not make any personal effort to obey God, then we presume upon His mercy and our proclaimed faith is nothing more than selfish presumption.

Through His saving blood Jesus reconciles us to His holy commandments. Once we come to understand this, the theme of our life will be "Oh, how I love Thy law!" even though all the while we will mournfully recognize that we fall woefully short of actually carrying out its demands. This is a normal Christian experience that we must recognize both intellectually and experientially.

Sanctification . . . a needed change

In understanding the liberating message of salvation through justification alone, there is a danger that we will become so en-

174

thusiastic about the idea that we will end up going to the other extreme and denying the proper role of biblical sanctification. It seems that today we hear much about righteousness by faith, while at the same time, a commitment to adhering to Bible standards is declining in the church. But this is not the way it should be. Those who truly embrace the life-changing message of God's love will seek to bring their lives into greater conformity to Christlike living. "They will always be trying to find out what best pleases the Lord" (Ephesians 5:10, Twentieth Century Translation). "Those who feel the constraining love of God, do not ask how little may be given to meet the requirements of God; they do not ask for the lowest standard, but aim at perfect conformity to the will of their Redeemer" (*Steps to Christ*, 45).

It's true that faith in the substitutionary death of Jesus is the only thing that can bring us the gift of salvation. But amazing transformations can be effected in people's lives through sanctification. "If men are willing to be molded, there will be brought about [by the power of the Holy Spirit] a sanctification of the whole being" (*Acts of the Apostles*, 53). As we place ourselves, by faith, in a right relationship with God through justification, we will miraculously come to love the things we once hated and hate the things we once loved. "If anyone is in Christ [justification], he is a new creation; The old has gone, the new has come!" (2 Corinthians 5:17, NIV).

Often here is where the devil trips us up right from the start by telling us that until we see all traces of the old man gone from our lives, then we really haven't become a new creature. But as justification deals the death blow to the old man of sin, the process by which he actually dies within us is that lifetime process called sanctification. The apostle Paul testified about himself that he was "always bearing about in the body the dying of the Lord Jesus, that the life also of Jesus might be made manifest in our body" (2 Corinthians 4:10, 11). This is the way it is, right up until the time when this "mortal shall have put on immortality" (1 Corinthians 15:54).

But, let's not miss the point that after justification there is a whole new direction to our life. A major radical change occurs. Instead of running *from* God, we're running *to* Him. Before, God and His ways used to seem tasteless. But now that we have tasted and seen that the Lord is good, we can't get enough of Him. Sanctification is higher than the highest human thought can reach. Yet it is also realistic. It ultimately has our complete recovery in mind—a recovery that we shall finally attain when the finishing touches of immortality are applied at the second coming of the One who began it all in us. Until that point, we continue to grow more like Him. And we grow with the same determination and focus that a plant grows in our garden—to bear fruit (see Mark 4:28). There are different stages in the growth process. And every plant is considered perfect at every stage, although it grows at a different rate. However, if a plant ever ceases to grow, it dies. So there's no stopping place, no cut off point. We must either grow or die.

So it is with Bible sanctification. We must be growing and making positive changes. And we know that! Though sometimes we may not see the growth that we would like to see, yet if we're trusting and being honest with ourselves, squarely facing our faults and imperfections, then God will see to it that we do grow and reach the desired end of being fruitful. Yet, we must never forget that all the while we are experiencing these "growing pains" in this imperfect state of human existence, we are at the same time complete in Christ because of our faith in the merits He gained for us at Calvary.

Such gospel realities are "the power of God unto salvation" (Romans 1:16). And if vividly grasped by the imagination, they will produce life within us. They will empower us to resist the devil, draw nigh to God, flee from lusts, and grow up into Christ. We will be more mature, less harmful, and more capable of having a positive, genuinely holy influence on others. We will become to them a little Garden of Eden, with the tree of life in the midst thereof, because we can more effectively lead them to a saving relationship with Jesus. We will become channels of light and not darkness.

As we determine to avoid the evils of this world, "denying ungodliness and worldly lusts," we become like Christian in John Bunyan's classic, *Pilgrim's Progress*. We will be constantly reaching out for that better country wherein our precious Lord resides. Abandoning all, our cry is "Life! Life! Eternal life!" with Him and through Him.

The golden standard

Make no mistake about it, God challenges us to be all we can be. Like Paul, we can choose to accept this stimulating offer and let Christ work in us "mightily" (Colossians 1:29). And, by the way, the standard we are to be striving to reach is none other than the golden rule. All the other attainments that God desires for us as individuals and as a church are simply to help us become more positive and effective Christian witnesses. To help us "do unto others" by revealing to them, through us, "the way, the truth, and the life" (John 14:6).

As we begin to apply this golden rule in our lives, we start to see how great a natural aversion we have to it—especially as it relates to those who are a threat to us, our enemies. This is because the golden rule means adapting ourselves to other people's experiences, which generally are totally unlike ours and foreign to us. But if we want to become effective in reaching others for Christ, we have to learn to treat others as we ourselves would want to be treated. Each person has a unique life experience that is essentially different from all others, and we need to be attuned to these needs and perspectives so that we can relate to each person in the way that will appeal to him most.

Such an attitude of caring does not come natural to our human hearts. That's why we tend to throw out a blanket standard that we expect everyone to live by. It's much easier to deal with everyone at the particular level with which we ourselves have become comfortable. And we can detect our unstable, carnal nature by the fact that *we* want to be the one who determines just what that blanket standard should be! In music, in dress, in diet, and even in matters of conscience as to how one worships God, we tend to make our opinions and interpretations of inspired counsels the rule for everyone around us. Yet while we parade our supposed holiness in these outward conformities, we often tend to neglect the "weightier matters of the law," particularly "mercy" (Matthew 23:23) in dealing with others in accordance with the golden rule.

God's standard is so much higher and more detailed than we might have ever supposed. Imagine reaching the point that you spend your time pondering the life of someone you can't stand, not for the purpose of judging or condemning him or her but in an effort to come up with some plan to help that person. Of course, this means constantly fighting back negative thoughts about that person while simultaneously straining to discover his or her good qualities. Imagine being able to meet others with whom you disagree and whom you suspect might even be an enemy to your faith, yet accepting them without fear that they are children of the devil sent to deceive you. Imagine divesting yourself of all this spiritual paranoia and actually being able to help them instead of turning them away in denunciation. This is freedom! "Perfect love casteth out fear" (1 John 4:18). And we can have this freedom. We can actually experience it as we become more and more sanctified.

But, if we ever hope to come to the place where we truly esteem others better than ourselves (see Philippians 2:3), we must learn from the One who was "meek and lowly in heart" (Matthew 11:29). This is how Jesus treated us. He followed the golden rule and became one of us through the Incarnation. And this was no short-term sacrifice. He identified Himself with humanity forever, throughout eternity! He is the Master of the art of practicing the golden rule. He's the One from whom Moses learned it. That's why Israel's leader finally came to the place that he was more concerned about the welfare of those in the church who disagreed with him than he was about his own eternal well-being. He said "Lord, blot my name out of the book, but let them live." And we can obtain that same kind of love from the same source from which Moses obtained it. "Learn of me," Jesus says to us (Matthew 11:29).

Practicing the golden rule is to be our lifework if we truly desire to be good, law-abiding citizens of God's government throughout the universe. But in order for us to practice the art successfully, we must first identify with others and become a ministering spirit to them, sympathizing with them concerning those things that are crushing out their lives. And we can't fake it. We must have a genuine interest in them. We must mentally put ourselves in their place. The true standard toward which God asks us to strive is not just the standards that we come up with from His inspired writings. It's not just about what we eat or wear or our forms of outward behavior. These things have their place. But God's highest calling is for us to break out of our self-centered thoughts and employ that brain power in doing good to those whom He places in our pathway. Any supposed standard of sanctification that falls short of this is a deception and a diversion from true godliness. As Martin Luther so aptly put it: "Faith receives the good works of Christ; love does good works for its neighbor."

In the blood from the cross
I have been washed from sin;
But to be free from dross,
Still I would enter in.
Day by day, hour by hour,
Blessings are sent to me;

SAVING BLOOD

But for more of His power
Ever my prayer shall be.
Near to Christ I would live,
Following Him each day;
What I ask He will give;
So then with faith I pray.
Now I have peace, sweet peace,
While in this world of sin;
But to pray I'll not cease
Till I am pure within.
Deeper yet, deeper yet,
Into the crimson flood;
Deeper yet, deeper yet,
Under the precious blood.

                    Johnson Oatman, Jr.

Conclusion

The Crescendo of Adventism

It has often been quoted in Adventist circles that "we have nothing to fear for the future, except as we shall forget the way the Lord has led us, and His teaching in our past history" (*Life Sketches*, 196). In this book we have looked at the great controversy between Christ and Satan, examining more closely the character, government, and purposes of each (see *The Great Controversy*, 593). It could very well be that the controversy will come to a climax in our day, ushering in both its final fury and its eternal glory. In contemplating this, let's go back and review just how God has been leading His people in the past. In doing so, we will gain fresh visions of how He is seeking to lead the church in the future. Hope, faith, and courage will replace doubt, fear, and unbelief, and we will be better equipped to meet the battles ahead.

We have studied how the angel Lucifer fell from his exalted position in heaven through his "ambition to be equal with God" and that "by the same means he seeks to cause the ruin of man" (*Testimonies for the Church*, 5:702). Satan caused the fall of the human race by causing our first parents to shift their focus from God to themselves—what would take place in them if they ate the forbidden fruit. This established a carnal nature in humanity that leads us to be self-focused instead of God-focused. And it has been by keeping us focused on ourselves instead of on God that the fallen rebel has been so successful in keeping the human race in bondage to sin.

When God brought the gospel to Adam and Eve (see Genesis 3:15), He called attention to the "enmity" between mankind and Satan that He would bring about by becoming incarnate in humanity. He emphasized this in an attempt to refocus the attention of Adam and Eve from themselves to Himself as their only hope of a cure. This was also the same lesson that He was trying to teach Israel in the wilderness by means of the bronze serpent on the pole. As long as the people kept their eyes on the serpent, which represented Christ, they were in the healing process. If, for any reason, they lost sight of the serpent and focused their attention on themselves or others, they fell back into the dying process.

The sanctuary services were also instituted in an effort to get men and women to look to God as the sole hope of their salvation. The lamb and the priesthood were symbols to teach the simple lesson that men and women needed to look only to Christ for the establishment of their righteousness and for mediation. But by the time of the Messiah's advent, the devil had managed to direct the emphasis of the tabernacle services from God and His righteousness and place it upon the righteousness and mediation of the human priests. The self-centered rules of the Pharisees had eclipsed humanity's views of God's holiness and led to the desecration of the golden rule within Israel. Israel believed that one established his righteousness through a system of human works. By receiving this principle of creature worship under the guise of authentic religion, Israel had once again taken its eyes off God and had placed them upon themselves. Though called of God to share the gospel with the world and thus bring in "everlasting righteousness," they themselves were now incapable of understanding the way of salvation (see Daniel 9:24).

By coming to His people, the Lord Jesus counteracted the devil's deception by calling Israel's attention back to God. He told Nicodemus, "as Moses lifted up the serpent in the wilderness, even so must the Son of man be lifted up: that whosoever believeth in him should not perish, but have everlasting life" (John 3:14, 15). And in John 12:32, Jesus declared "I, if I be lifted up from the earth, will draw all men unto me." It was at Calvary that He was literally "lifted up from the earth." Through His ministry, Jesus had caught the attention of many people and centered their gaze once more on God as their only hope. His death temporarily dashed their hopes. By killing Christ, Satan had sought once again to remove Him from the creature's view. This is symbolized by Mary Magdelene's sorrowful statement, "They have taken away my Lord, and I know not where they have laid him" (John 20:13). But after Jesus' resurrection, His followers understood that by His death at Calvary He had paid the debt sin had incurred. Now, by faith in the merits of His righteousness, they could be found righteous in Him.

This was the burden of the gospel in the apostolic church— to wean humanity's hope from itself and center it upon "Jesus Christ, and him crucified" (1 Corinthians 2:2). The apostle Paul understood that his only hope of salvation was to "be found in him [Jesus], not having mine own righteousness, which is of the law, but that which is through the faith of Christ, the righteousness which is of God by faith" (Philippians 3:9). But Paul went on to warn of those who were "enemies of the cross of Christ," who did not look to Christ as their only hope of being made righteous. Instead, the apostle said, they "mind earthly things," that is, they have their focus on this fallen earth and its fallen creatures. But Paul reminded the followers of Christ that "our conversation [citizenship] is in heaven; from whence also we look for the Saviour, the Lord Jesus Christ" (verses 19, 20).

The early church's attention was once again directed heavenward by its understanding that Christ had ascended to the sanctuary above to enter upon His role as High Priest. By keeping their focus on Him there, and the work He was doing in ministering His mediatorial merits in their behalf, the disciples' faith grew strong. Consequently, it was but a matter of time before they received the Holy Spirit's power at Pentecost and set the world ablaze with the gospel truth. Christ's merits and His intercessory work as High Priest was the burden of the book of Hebrews.

As the early church directed the world's attention to Christ in heaven, the devil was challenged once again to find a way to remove Christ from central focus. The Lord had actually foretold his plan of attack through Daniel's vision of the "little horn" in Daniel, chapter 8. It was no longer possible for Satan to corrupt the priesthood, for Jesus was the priest, and the sanctuary was in heaven. So, he did the next best thing. He counterfeited Christ's high priestly role by instituting another earthly sanctuary through the little-horn power.

As the early church leaders died and passed off the scene, Satan worked through men who desired to "draw away disciples after them" (Acts 20:30). Through this means he would eventually institute the papal mass. Instead of confessing their sins to their High Priest in heaven, people were now taught to make human beings their confessors. In place of trusting solely to Christ's merits as their only hope of forgiveness, people were led to trust in their own meritorious works and to those of their fellow creatures, the "saints." Through the papal religion, "the place of his [God's] sanctuary was cast down," and once again, by diverting minds from the work of Christ in heaven and focusing it back to this earth, the little horn "practised, and prospered" (Daniel 8:11, 12). Having eclipsed the light shining on the earth from the Sun of Righteousness, the world was plunged into the Dark Ages. Thus again the creature "exalted himself above all that is called God, or that is worshipped; so that he as God sitteth in the temple of God, shewing himself that he is God" (2 Thessalonians 2:4). He boldly usurped God's authority as both Creator and Redeemer—as well as the biblical Sabbath that serves as a reminder of that authority. The institution of Sunday sacredness, in place of the seventh-day Sabbath, serves as a memorial to the creature's independence from the "Lord . . . of the sabbath" (Mark 2:28).

But God would not give up the battle. He had promised men and women that He would stick with them to the end of the world. The dawning rays of the Reformation's light was to greatly stir a world that had been sleeping in darkness. The Catholic doctrine of justification taught that a person becomes righteous as a result of combining Christ's merits with his own obedient works. By the Holy Spirit's influence on the heart, it is taught, human beings can themselves become "inwardly just" (*Catechism of the Catholic Church*, 1996, 536). This subtle doctrine, though apparently placing a high value on the work of the Holy Spirit, actually led the creature to focus on himself for evidence of righteousness, rather than to rely entirely on the righteousness of Christ in his behalf.

This futile search for inward righteousness finally led Martin Luther to conclude that "the just shall live by faith" (Romans 1:17). Thus the major principle of the Protestant Reformation had been laid—that human beings can put no "confidence in the flesh" (Philippians 3:3). Luther accurately taught that even the obedience and good works wrought out in us by the Holy Spirit were unclean if the covering cloud of grace is removed. This teaching began to cause men and women to look away from themselves and focus on Christ and His intercessory merits as their only hope of being accounted righteous.

The undoing of the Reformation

Unfortunately, as the reformers began to experience conflicts and struggles among themselves, they began focusing on the supposed faults and errors of each other. And, of course, the mind that is focused on another's faults can't possibly remain firmly focused on God and His righteousness. "It is Satan's constant effort to keep the attention diverted from the Saviour and thus prevent the union and communion of the soul with Christ. The pleasures of the world, life's cares and perplexities and sorrows, the faults of others, or your own faults and imperfections—to any or all of these he will seek to divert the mind" (*Steps to Christ*, 71). Because of inner conflicts among the leaders of the Reformation, this great liberating movement began to break down.

But God had no intention of not finishing what He had started. The flame He ignited through the Reformation was destined to illuminate the entire world with the knowledge of God. As that flame again began to burn low, the Lord pitched some additional fuel on it by leading William Miller to discover the ancient time prophecy of Daniel 8:14. The force behind Miller's message was the historical accuracy of the dates contained in Daniel's 2,300 day prophecy (see Daniel, chapters 8, 9). Miller concluded that the events there predicted would take place sometime around 1843 or 1844. However, the weakness of the message proclaimed by Miller and his counterparts was that their focus was again on this earth instead of heaven. They reasoned that the sanctuary to be cleansed was the earth. Thus the disappointment was inevitable, as is always the case when our focus is earthward and not heavenward.

But the disappointment was only temporary. Through a an illumination of Hiram Edson in a New York cornfield, God was continuing to restore to the church what it had lost through the papal apostasy—advanced knowledge of where Jesus was and what He was doing. This revelation had the potential to take God's people into the kingdom just shortly after 1844.

So the devil got busy and brought about many fanatical movements among the remnant people of God. Spiritualistic theories began to be promoted, confusing the mind about both the nature of God and man. Along with these false views, Satan managed to get the early advent pioneers to place their focus of the three angels' messages on a human obedience to the law instead of on the merits of Christ through the "everlasting gospel" (Revelation 14:6). This trend of focusing on the creature's efforts to keep the law continued to grow in the church until the fateful year of 1888. It was then that Ellen White announced to the church that it had preached the law until it had become as dry as the hills of Gilboa.

Then, in the 1888 General Conference session held at Minneapolis, the Lord sent His people a precious message through Waggoner and Jones. It attempted to shift Adventists' focus back to the gospel. But the message of Christ's righteousness met heavy resistance from well-meaning, conservative ranks within the church. This group had become accustomed to trusting to a righteousness it believed was established by obedience to the law, through the process of sanctification. Like Israel of old, "they being ignorant of God's righteousness, and going about to establish their own righteousness, had not submitted themselves unto the righteousness of God" (Romans 10:3).

As a result, the church missed another opportunity, as did Israel, to "bring in everlasting righteousness" (Daniel 9:24). That's why Ellen White declared in 1901, "We may have to remain here in this world because of insubordination many more years, as did the children of Israel" (*Evangelism*, 696).

Adventism getting it together

When the creature trusts to his own right doing as evidence of his own righteousness, he makes himself into a god, because he trusts to what he is doing as a means of saving himself. Rarely, of course, will individuals adopt such a blatant doctrine of legalism. Therefore, the devil has to present the same principle in a more subtle manner.

Astonishingly, some within Adventism teach, in essence, a Catholic version of the doctrine of justification by faith. Such believe that by the process of sanctification we are to be literally made righteous in this life. Though they give the Holy Spirit credit for this work, the end result is the same—the focus is taken away from Christ and His righteousness. To substitute the good work that the Holy Spirit does in our lives for the work Christ did at the Cross in our behalf serves only the devil's purpose. It undermines total dependence upon Christ and causes us to look within for evidence of righteousness.

But the church has not only had to guard against an extreme view of sanctification; it also has to remain on guard against an extreme view of justification. Extreme justification teaches that everyone was legally justified at the Cross, even though they may still have an attitude of rebellion against God. Such a doctrine actually affirms the creature in his self-worship by providing him the full benefits of Calvary's atoning act even before he repents!

Despite these opposite extremes in the church, it's exciting that the mainstream theology of our denomination is moving in the right direction. Once we understand and accept that the denominational core believes and teaches the balanced view of salvation taught in the Bible, everything falls into place. We are no longer at war in our hearts with the church and its leadership. Criticism and condemnation is replaced with confidence that God is leading the church, and we find in our hearts a corresponding golden-rule attitude toward its leaders. Personal pride and ideas of self-sufficiency are crucified. As we come to trust solely in the merits of Christ for the establishment of any righteousness in this life, we lay down the heavy burden of trying to become good enough to be saved; we find rest for our souls. This, of course, gives true meaning to the Sabbath, as we enter into the rest of relying in Christ's merits (see Hebrews 4:10). It brings our understanding of the three angels' messages full circle. It connects the Sabbath of the Creator to the rest we find in the security of the everlasting gospel. And all this rivets our focus on Christ as our only source of righteousness. And when the church puts all these elements together, you get the loud cry!

But the church must not expect to herald this precious

message without a challenge from both within and without. To-day, some inside the church are rising up against the gospel because they feel the heavy emphasis on justification leads to a lowering of standards. But justification actually leads to *higher* standards in the lives of those who truly receive it by faith in Christ. Faith in Christ's substitutionary merits is the victory that brings to the soul power to overcome the world.

Hanging upon the cross Christ was the gospel. Now we have a message, "Behold the Lamb of God, which taketh away the sins of the world." Will not our church members keep their eyes fixed on a crucified and risen Saviour, in whom their hopes of eternal life are centered? This is our message, our argument, our doctrine, our warning to the inpenitent, our encouragement for the sorrowing, the hope for every believer. If we can awaken an interest in men's minds that will cause them to fix their eyes on Christ, we may step aside, and ask them only to continue to fix their eyes upon the Lamb of God. They thus receive their lesson. Whosoever will come after Me, let him deny himself, and take up his cross, and follow Me. He whose eyes are fixed on Jesus will leave all. He will die to selfishness. He will believe in all the Word of God, which is so gloriously and wonderfully exalted in Christ. As the sinner sees Jesus as He is, an all compassionate Saviour, hope and assurance take possession of his soul. The helpless soul is cast without any reservation upon Jesus. None can bear away from the vision of Christ Jesus crucified a lingering doubt. Unbelief is gone (*Manuscript Releases*, 21:37).

And remember, it was unbelief that kept the children of Israel out of the Promised Land (see Hebrews 3:19). "Let us labour therefore to enter into that rest [of relying on Christ's righteous merits], lest any man fall after the same example of unbelief" (Hebrews 4:11). Are not these things "written for our admonition?" (1 Corinthians 10:11).

This has been the real core of the struggle throughout the history of the church on earth—to keep the eyes fixed on Christ and His merits as our only hope. It is the only hope of humanity making any real progress. "He who is trying to reach heaven by his own works in keeping the law, is attempting an impossibility. . . . When we seek to gain heaven through the merits of Christ, the soul makes progress" (*Review and Herald*, 1 July 1890).

Justification by faith in the saving blood of Calvary's Lamb shook the first family when it tested Cain and Abel. That same message shook the Israelites on the borders of Caanan. Justification again shook the Jewish nation during the time of Christ and His apostles. Luther proclaimed it and nearly shook the church of Rome to her knees. Justification through Christ's righteousness shook the Adventist Church in 1888. And what is even more sobering, that message ended up shaking even the Minneapolis messengers who presented it! There is no doubt that the message of the justifying blood of Christ, as it relates to the immutability of God's law as seen in the Sabbath commadment, will shake the whole world in the end time (see Hebrews 12).

Soon there will be only two religions in all the world—man's religion and God's religion. There will soon be only two types of worshipers—those who trust their own righteousness and those who trust solely in Christ's righteousness. Everyone will be represented either by the Pharisee or the publican, by Cain or Abel.

> Cain and Abel represent two classes that will exist in the world till the close of time. *One class will avail themselves of the appointed sacrifice for sin; the other venture to depend upon their own merits;* theirs is a sacrifice without the virtue of divine mediation, and thus it is not able to bring man into favor with God. . . . Both

[Cain and Abel] were sinners, and both acknowledged the claims of God to reverence and worship. To outward appearance their religion was the same up to a certain point, but beyond this the difference between the two was great (*Patriarchs and Prophets*, 72, 73, 72).

By faith Abel offered unto God a more excellent sacrifice than Cain, by which he obtained witness that he was righteous, God testifying of his gifts: and by it he being dead yet speaketh (Hebrews 11:4).

He that hath an ear, let him hear what the Spirit saith unto the churches (Revelation 3:22).

We all need the saving blood of Christ.

The church has one foundation, 'Tis Jesus Christ her Lord;
She is His new creation, By water and the word;
From heaven He came and sought her, To be His holy bride;
With His own blood He bought her, And for her life He died.

Elect from every nation, Yet one o'er all the earth;
Her charter of salvation, One Lord, one faith, one birth;
One holy name she blesses, Partakes one holy food,
And to one hope she presses, With every grace endued.

Though with a scornful wonder, Men see her sore oppressed,
Though foes would rend asunder, The Rock where she doth rest,
Yet saints their faith are keeping; Their cry goes up, "How long?"
And soon the night of weeping, Shall be the morn of song.

Samuel J. Stone

If you enjoyed this book, you'll enjoy these as well:

The Gift
*Kim Allan Johnson.*An unforgettable look at the sacrifice of Christ.
The Gift, by Kim Allan Johnson, will put you back in touch with the
God who would rather go to hell for you than to live in heaven
without you.
0-8163-1768-2. Paperback. US$11.99, Cdn$17.99

By His Stripes
Clifford Goldstein. A passionate, sometimes shocking, reexamination
of the Great Controversy and the glory of redemption through the
gospel of Isaiah—a book that has more to say about God's love,
creation, free will, salvation, justice and righteousness—than almost
any other book of the Bible. 0-8163-1699-6. Hardcover. US$17.99,
Cdn$26.99.

Stand at the Cross and Be Changed
E. Lonnie Melashenko and *John Thomas McLarty.*Who were the
people gathered at the foot of the cross the day Jesus died? What
were their thoughts? Through the pages of *Stand at the Cross and Be
Changed*, join those who watched the Saviour die. This powerful
book by Lonnie Melashenko, speaker/director of the *Voice of Prophecy*, revisits the greatest event in human history through the eyes of
those gathered at Golgotha and through the last words of Christ.
0-8163-1384-9. Paper. US$8.99, Cdn$13.49.

Order from your ABC by calling **1-800-765-6955**, or get on-line and
shop our virtual store at **www.adventistbookcenter.com**.

Read a chapter from your favorite book

Order online

Sign up for e-mail notices on new products